Date Due

JUN 6 1986			
DEC 29 1989			
NOV 26 1993			
MAR 21 1997			
JUL 26 2001			
DEC - 5 2001			

BRODART, INC.   Cat. No. 23 233   Printed in U.S.A.

TWAYNE'S WORLD AUTHORS SERIES
A Survey of the World's Literature

Sylvia E. Bowman, Indiana University
GENERAL EDITOR

SPAIN

Gerald Wade, Vanderbilt University
Janet W. Díaz, University of North Carolina, Chapel Hill
EDITORS

Tirso de Molina

TWAS 445

Courtesy of The Hispanic Society of America

Tirso de Molina

TIRSO DE MOLINA

By MARGARET WILSON
The University of Hull

TWAYNE PUBLISHERS
A DIVISION OF G. K. HALL & CO. BOSTON

Copyright © 1977 by G. K. Hall & Co.
All Rights Reserved

Library of Congress Cataloging in Publication Data

Wilson, Margaret, 1921 (Aug. 22)–
  Tirso de Molina.

  (Twayne's world authors series; TWAS 445: Spain)
  Bibliography: p. 155–58.
  Includes index.
  1. Téllez, Gabriel, 1570?–1648—Criticism and
interpretation.
  PQ6436.W54   862'.3   77-5947
  ISBN 0-8057-6181-7

PQ
6436
.W54

MANUFACTURED IN THE UNITED STATES OF AMERICA

To the Memory of My Parents

Contents

About the Author
Preface
Chronology
1. Tirso's Life   13
2. Tirso's Theater   30
3. Intrigue and Illusion   45
4. Countryside and Capital   57
5. Oddities and Outsiders   66
6. Forgiveness and Friendship   78
7. Monarchs and Ministers   86
8. Saints and Sinners   98
9. Salvation and Damnation   109
10. Other Works   126
11. Conclusion   136
    Notes and References   145
    Selected Bibliography   155
    Index   159

About the Author

Margaret Wilson is a Senior Lecturer in Spanish at the University of Hull. She studied at Cambridge University, and subsequently held lecturing posts in the Universities of Leeds and Manchester before joining the Hull staff in 1963.

Margaret Wilson's publications include articles on Tirso de Molina and other dramatists, and a Critical Guide to the poems of San Juan de la Cruz. Her book *Spanish Drama of the Golden Age* is widely used by English-speaking students. She is currently (1975–77) President of the Association of Hispanists of Great Britain and Ireland.

Preface

To present in a limited space the work of an author as prolific as Tirso de Molina one must either generalize or select. I have chosen to select, and in this study have analyzed no more than half of his fifty-odd extant authentic plays, less than a third of those that at one time or another have been attributed to him. Faced with so much material no two critics would make precisely the same choice, and those already familiar with Tirso's theater may well be sorry to find certain plays excluded; I myself regret not having been able to make room for *La villana de Vallecas, La república al revés, La mejor espigadera, Escarmientos para el cuerdo,* and several others. Nevertheless all the major works receive attention, and the lesser known plays studied are, I hope, as representative as possible. I have included one or two mediocre pieces, even at the cost of omitting better ones, because they seemed more typical of certain aspects of Tirso's drama.

The categories in which I have grouped the plays are not mutually exclusive, as is apparent from the fact that *La venganza de Tamar (Tamar's Vengeance)* figures in two chapters. A number of the plays dealt with later in the book are as much comedies of intrigue as those of Chapter 3, and it is not only in the plays of Chapter 7 that typical *privado* figures are to be found. The chapter headings are intended to indicate aspects of Tirso's theater rather than a rigid categorization of his plays. The disproportionate length of Chapters 1 and 2 reflects the complexity of the biographical and bibliographical problems that still exercise Tirsian scholars.

All references to the plays are to the three-volume edition by Blanca de los Ríos of Tirso's *Obras dramáticas completas.* Volume and page number are given for the first reference to a play in each chapter, thereafter page number alone; the letter a or b after the page number indicates first or second column. Quotations appear in translation only, apart from a few instances in the Conclusion where the Spanish wording is relevant. Similarly, in accordance with the norms of the Twayne series, titles are given in Spanish and English on their early occurrences and thereafter in translation only. It is hoped that this may make Tirso's work a little more accessible to the general reader who has no Spanish, and that Hispanist scholars and students will not be too irked by the need to translate back to the forms with which they are familiar. Titles are rendered literally whenever the result seems acceptable in English; I have occasionally settled for a slightly freer version where this sounded more like a genuine English title, for example, "Enough is as Good as a Feast" instead of "Too much is as bad as too little," and "The Man of Little Faith" rather than "The man damned for lack of faith."

My indebtedness to many other critics will be apparent. Among living writers on Tirso I should particularly like to mention Manuel Penedo, Serge Maurel and André Nougué, Alan Paterson and Daniel Rogers, and above all Ruth Lee Kennedy and Gerald E. Wade. These last two scholars, *tirsistas* of much longer and much higher standing than myself, have both helped me immeasurably in my writing of this book, generously supplying me with their publications, with information of various kinds, and with unfailing encouragement. I only hope that they will not find the resulting work too inadequate a tribute to the subject of our common interest.

I am very grateful to Professor Janet W. Díaz, the present Spanish editor of the series, for helpful advice, and to my colleagues of the Department of Hispanic Studies in the University of Hull for enabling me to take the term's study leave during which the greater part of the book was written; I particularly appreciate the help and kindness of the head of the department, Professor C. B. Morris, who so readily undertook lecturing on my behalf. And to no one am I more indebted than to Miss Jill Hodgson, the secretary of the department, who has typed the whole of my text with meticulous accuracy and neatness, and with the most willing cooperation. To her, as to all others who have helped me in any way, I express my warmest thanks.

MARGARET WILSON

University of Hull

Chronology

1580 or 1581	Gabriel Téllez born in Madrid.
1601	Professed in the order of our Lady of Mercy (Mercedarian order) at Guadalajara.
1601–1610	Studies in Salamanca, Toledo, Guadalajara, and Alcalá.
1610–1611	In Madrid. Begins to write for the theater.
1611–1615	In Toledo.
1616	Begins to use the pseudonym of "Tirso de Molina."
1616–1618	Takes part in the mission of his order to Santo Domingo in the West Indies.
1618–1620	In Segovia; in the latter year receives title of *Presentado* in his order. In 1620 or 1621 moves to Madrid, and begins his major period of literary activity.
1624	Publishes *Los cigarrales de Toledo* (*The Country Houses of Toledo*).
1625	Censured by the *Junta de reformación* (Committee for Reform), and forced to leave Madrid.
1626–1629	*Comendador* of the Mercedarian monastery in Trujillo.
1627	First *parte* of his plays published in Seville.
1629	In Salamanca. Organizes a literary competition in honor of the canonization of two Mercedarian saints.
1630	His Act of Contrition published in Madrid.
1630–1632	In Toledo.
1631 or 1632	Appointed chronicler of the Mercedarian order.
1632	Appointed *Definidor* in the Castilian province of the order. Spends next eight years in Madrid.
1634	Third *parte* of his plays published in Tortosa.
1635	Second and Fourth *partes*, and *Deleitar aprovechando* (*Pleasure with Profit*), published in Madrid.

1636	Fifth *parte* published in Madrid.
1639	Completes *Historia general de la Orden de Nuestra Señora de las Mercedes* (*History of the Mercedarian Order*). Awarded title of *Maestro*.
1640	Censured by Salmerón and sent to Cuenca.
1645	Appointed *Comendador* in Soria.
1648	Died in Almazán.

CHAPTER 1

Tirso's Life

ALTHOUGH the Spanish Golden Age theater may be said to have come into being in the 1580s with the first plays of Lope de Vega, and to have survived until the death of Calderón in 1681, most of the plays by which it is now remembered date from a relatively short period of some thirty years in the middle of that century span. It was only in middle age or later that Lope produced his dramatic masterpieces; he may be said to dominate the decade of the 1610s. Most of Calderón's major works for the public theaters date from the 1630s. Both these dramatists were also at work in the twenties, but this intervening decade, or at least the first half of it, sees above all the predominance of Tirso de Molina. He claimed in 1621 to have written three hundred plays during the preceding fourteen years, and in the four that followed he was to write many more, including some of his most memorable works. Yet this prolific writer, one of the three outstanding Spanish dramatists of his age, had by the nineteenth century dwindled into a shadowy figure about whose life very little was known.

I *When was Tirso born?*

The only facts never lost from view were that "Tirso de Molina" was a pseudonym, his real name being Gabriel Téllez; that he was a native of Madrid; that he became a monk in the Mercedarian order, and died in 1648. When the bicentenary of his death was marked by the publication in 1848 of a volume of his plays in the *Biblioteca de autores españoles,* the critics who contributed forewords were strikingly at variance over the age at which he entered the cloister, and even over the year in which he was born. Durán conjectured that this must have been around 1570, Javier de Burgos hazarded only some time in the last quarter of the sixteenth century, and Meso-

13

nero Romanos stated with rather more assurance that it was about 1585.

In 1885 the Spanish Academy organized a competition with the aim of bringing to light new facts about this major but elusive dramatist. No entry falling within the stated terms was received, and no prize was awarded; but the challenge served as a stimulus to two men who, one in the field of literary criticism and the other in that of biography and editorship, were to initiate a new phase of Tirsian scholarship. Pedro Muñoz Peña's *El teatro de Tirso de Molina* (Valladolid, 1889) was a pioneer literary study, although now outdated; Emilio Cotarelo's *Tirso de Molina: Investigaciones bio-bibliográficas* (Madrid, 1893), coming nearer to the Academy's intention, began to sketch an outline of Tirso's career. On the date of birth Cotarelo adduced as evidence an eighteenth-century portrait of the dramatist (then in private hands, now in the National Library in Madrid), with an inscription stating that he was born in 1572, and died on 12 March 1648 aged seventy-six years and five months. There is obviously some inaccuracy here, as Cotarelo realized, since a man dying at that age in March 1648 must have been born in the autumn of 1571. Cotarelo searched in vain in the parish registers of Madrid for some entry that would resolve the doubt; but at all events the portrait supported Durán's suggestion of a date of birth around 1570, and this became generally accepted.

The academicians must have been surprised to discover that they had also inspired the interest of a young woman. Blanca de los Ríos had been from childhood an avid reader of Golden Age drama, and she now defied the restrictive social conventions of her day to begin her own investigations in libraries and archives, thus embarking on a long lifetime of Tirsian research. Her first findings were published in 1910 in a book of essays, *Del Siglo de Oro (On the Golden Age)*; but it was not until 12 November 1922 that she announced in an article in the newspaper *ABC* a new development concerning the date of Tirso's birth. A Mercedarian monk from Chile, Fray Pedro Nolasco Pérez, had discovered in the Archives of the Indies in Seville the royal authorization for a party of monks to travel to the West Indies in 1616. Tirso, or rather Fray Gabriel Téllez, was one of this party, and was listed as being thirty-three years old. This would fix his birth in 1583, a date much nearer that suggested by Mesonero Romanos than the 1572 of the portrait.

II *The Theory of Blanca de los Ríos*

Clearly more investigation was required; so Blanca de los Ríos went again to the parish registers, but this time to those covering the early 1580s. It was in the church of San Ginés that she found what she was looking for, the record of the baptism of a child named Gabriel. The parents were given as Gracia Juliana and an unknown father; the godparents, witnesses and officiating priest were named, and the date was 9 March 1584. Doña Blanca was convinced that the entry related to Tirso. The discrepancy of a year from the date suggested by the document of 1616 could easily be accounted for: for instance, "thirty-three years of age" might mean "in his thirty-third year." There could no longer be any question of Tirso's having been born in the 1570s.

Moreover, the entry seemed to yield even more exciting information. In the margin the name Gabriel was repeated, followed by three lines heavily crossed out; and under the obliteration Doña Blanca claimed to read words meaning "Téllez Girón, son of the duke of Osuna." If this was so, the unknown father of Gabriel was in fact one of the foremost noblemen of the realm. Here was a story to add color and relief to the hitherto shadowy figure of the dramatist—indeed, to make of him something like a character from one of his own plays. If he was the unacknowledged son of a grandee, this would explain not merely the strange absence of any other concrete facts about his origins, but also the note of resentment that occurs more than once in his writings, and his obvious sympathy for those of his heroes whom Doña Blanca calls the "nameless sons"— the illegitimate offspring and the younger brothers, deprived of all the advantages of the ancestry they shared with their more fortunate kin.

Despite this argument in its favor Blanca de los Ríos' thesis about Tirso's origins was on the whole skeptically received. Not all those who subsequently examined the baptismal entry agreed with her deciphering of it, and even her reading postulated some unlikely abbreviations. And weighty objections were put forward in 1949 by two Mercedarian monks, Miguel L. Ríos and Manuel Penedo, in a special number of the Mercedarian review *Estudios* brought out to mark the tercentenary of Tirso's death.[1] They pointed out firstly, that it was common, then as now, to adopt a new name on profession in the order, and that Gabriel may well not have been the name that Tirso received at the font; and secondly, that had he been illegitimate, he would have needed a special dispensation to be ordained priest and on the occasion of every new appointment within the order—but no record of any such dispensations exists. The majority of critics have agreed with these arguments and seen Doña Blanca's theory as fanciful.

Some, however, have lent it support. Mario Penna in 1958 reported his experiments with ultraviolet and infrared photographs of the baptismal entry. These unfortunately were inconclusive, but the blots on the opposite page, made when the register was closed with the ink still wet, might be thought to read "Osuna." Penna also maintained that if the house of Osuna was anxious to keep Tirso's origins dark by suppressing the dispensations for illegitimacy, it was certainly powerful enough to be able to do so.[2]

Undoubtedly the oddest support for Blanca de los Ríos came in a series of short articles published in an obscure provincial journal in 1951. They have received no publicity, and I owe my knowledge of them to the kindness of the distinguished Tirsian specialist Gerald E. Wade, who has let me have his copy. The author is one José Rus Lucenilla. He accepts that the child to whom the baptismal entry refers is the future Tirso de Molina and that the duke of Osuna was his father, and goes on to find identities among the high aristocracy of the time for all the others mentioned, the godparents and witnesses as well as the mother, Gracia Juliana. She would be the duke's third wife, but may not have married him until after the birth of Gabriel. Hence the secrecy surrounding the baptism, and the recording of the names of the participants in an abridged and unrecognizable form.[3] However, any credibility the identifications might have carried is forfeited by the complete absence of documentation. Professor Wade, who has an unrivaled knowledge of Spanish genealogy of the time, cannot confirm them, and confesses himself baffled by the articles. Rus Lucenilla, if he is indeed a genuine investigator, cannot be said to have shed any new light on the matter.

Recently Henry Sullivan has adopted, though more cautiously, the same expedient of examining the identity of other persons mentioned in the entry. One of the godparents is named as Gaspar Hidalgo, and Sullivan points to the novelist Gaspar Lucas Hidalgo,

Tirso's Life 17

who used the same Barcelona publisher as Tirso did on occasion, and one of whose collections served as a model for Tirso's miscellany *Deleitar aprovechando* (*Pleasure with Profit*). Was this fellow litterateur Tirso's godfather?[4] The suggestion is interesting, but not convincing.

III *The Document of 1638*

The latest document to be discovered is the one that probably carries most weight. Guillermo Guastavino reported in 1961 the discovery by E. Rodríguez Demorizi of a deposition made by Tirso himself on 25 January 1638, in which he stated that he was then fifty-seven years old.[5] This would place his birth in 1580 or early 1581. Presumably the dramatist's own evidence is the most reliable, and certainly more so than that of a baptismal entry which there are only flimsy grounds for believing to be his. Father Manuel Penedo, in the introduction to his recent edition of Tirso's *History of the Mercedarian Order*,[6] accepts the evidence of this document, and agrees with Guastavino's explanation of the discrepancy from the birth-date of 1583 suggested by the royal authorization of 1616: namely, that that collective passport recorded the ages of the monks who were to travel, not as they were on the date it was issued but as they had been when the information was first supplied, some considerable time beforehand. As Penedo realizes, that would imply that the information had been collected as early as 1614 and never brought up to date. I find this suggestion unlikely, since on Penedo's own showing there is no real evidence for the journey to the West Indies having been planned before 1615; but in any case, if it cannot be specified in what year it was that Tirso gave his age as thirty-three, then the 1616 document is of very little value as a guide to his date of birth. It seems safest to follow the 1638 deposition and to state that Tirso was born between 26 January 1580 and 25 January 1581—most probably, therefore, some time in the year 1580.[7]

IV *Tirso's Ancestry*

Nothing can be stated with any certainty about Tirso's family background. In his late fragment *La vida de Santa María de Cervellón* (*The Life of Santa María de Cervellón*) he declares himself to be a descendant of the principality of Catalonia. Penedo connects this claim with his pseudonym and suggests that Molina may in fact have been one of his family names, indicating a relationship with the overlords of the town of Molina de Aragón, who had links with Catalonia. Support for this idea may perhaps be seen in Tirso's exaltation of members of the Molina family in two important plays, *La prudencia en la mujer* (*Prudence in Woman*) and *Cómo han de ser los amigos* (*True Friendship*). His claim may however refer simply to Catalan origin, and not to noble blood. It is interesting that the Mercedarian order he chose to join was of Catalan foundation.

If Blanca de los Ríos' hypothesis is rejected, nothing at all is known of his parents. In *Los cigarrales de Toledo* (*The Country Houses of Toledo*) he mentions "a sister he had in his native town, his equal in talent and in misfortune";[8] and it was apparently a nephew of his, one Francisco Lucas de Avila, who collected a number of his plays for publication in the 1630s. In view of the uncertainties that have already been seen to cloud so many details of Tirso's life, it is not surprising to find that the existence of this nephew has often been questioned, on the grounds that the style of the prologues bearing his name is suspiciously like that of the dramatist himself. Yet as it was to him that the official license to print the fifth volume of plays was granted in 1636 he must presumably have been a real person, whatever his precise role in the enterprise. Penedo believes that it was a major one.

On Tirso's reference to the talent of his unnamed sister Ruth Lee Kennedy bases a suggestion that she may perhaps be identified with the nun, María de San Ambrosio y Piña, who contributed one of the laudatory verses that figure among the preliminaries to *Los cigarrales de Toledo* (*The Country Houses of Toledo*). The verse in question may be thought to be sisterly in tone, and addresses its recipient as Gabriel rather than by his literary pseudonym.[9] Penedo thinks this identification unlikely, since the sister would probably be the mother of Francisco Lucas de Avila and therefore not a nun. However, Tirso never says that he has only one sister; and these speculations are in any case of minor importance for a study of the dramatist himself.

The scene of *The Country Houses of Toledo* in which the sister is mentioned will repay a little further study. A kind of regatta is taking place, and Tirso himself is one of the competitors. He wins a prize, and in default of a lady on whom to bestow it sends it to his sister in Madrid. His entry is described thus:

Tirso's Life

Tirso, who although a humble shepherd of the Manzanares [i.e. the river on which Madrid stands], found in the generous openness of Toledo a more ready acceptance than in his native town—so dominated by envious outsiders—appeared in a small though ingeniously decorated boat, beflowered like a Hybla garden, and in the middle of it a very tall palm tree from whose topmost branches hung a crown of laurel. The shepherd climbed up toward it, wearing a white cloak with purple stripes on the breast, the sign of his profession, and borne up by two wings, the one inscribed "Talent" and the other "Study." With these he flew so high as to be able to touch the crown, even though Envy, in its usual guise of a snake, coiled at his feet, tried to prevent the triumphant accomplishment of his endeavors, although in vain, for trampling it underfoot he hung from the branches this sign, intended also for the judges: "Velis, nolis" [i.e. "Whether you like it or not"]. (I, 116)

There is a clear indication here of hostility on the part of some envious opponent, or opponents, whom Tirso is determined to outshine; but a tantalizing obscurity as regards identities. Since the envy seems to be centered in Madrid, and the sister who lives there is also unfortunate, Blanca de los Ríos deduces that the enmity was of a dynastic nature, and sees the passage as support for her theory of Tirso's noble but illegitimate birth.[10] His words would thus be a protest and warning to the family who ostracized him and his sister, and who, although established at court in Madrid, did not share his native ability or his capacity for hard work.

His claim to have received better treatment in Toledo certainly seems to be substantiated. *The Country Houses* is about the Toledan nobility and their pastimes, and André Nougué, in his major study of the work, shows that many of the characters can be identified with aristocrats of Tirso's own day;[11] the author clearly mixed with them on equal terms and was at home in their stately dwellings. Gerald E. Wade has carried the identifications much further, and through close comparative studies of the character names in many of Tirso's works and of the genealogies of the period, has reached the conclusion that the dramatist was on friendly terms with a number of Spain's leading families.[12] This in turn inclines him to believe that Tirso himself was probably of noble birth.

There are other possibilities, however. Ruth Lee Kennedy and Manuel Penedo each have their own candidate for the role of Tirso's unnamed adversary: the former believes the quarrel to have had its setting in the literary circles of the time; the latter places it within the Mercedarian order (see below, p. 26). Neither therefore sees the passage from *The Country Houses* as having any bearing on Tirso's ancestry. Professor Kennedy does not think that he needed noble blood to be received into Toledan society: "Toledo's elite had accepted Tirso as one of their own, their equal by virtue of his outstanding talent, his solid knowledge, his attractive personality, and his position in an old and honorable Order that received Philip III's favor"; and points out that Tirso calls himself a humble shepherd of the Manzanares precisely when stressing the open generosity he found in Toledo.[13] It is worth noting that he frequently applies the word "generous" to the upper classes without any moral connotation, simply to mean "aristocratic." He would seem, therefore, to be pointing the contrast between his own humble origins and the nobility of his hosts, just as much as that between Madrid and Toledo. Admittedly, in the reconstruction of Tirso's life one is often building on shifting ground, and his use of the word "humble" might possibly be ironical, hinting at some deprivation of rank. The most natural deduction, however, is that Tirso was socially speaking a nonentity, whose ability and application did indeed bear him aloft to the laurel wreath of fame.

V His Membership of the Mercedarian Order

The course of Tirso's adult life can fortunately be charted with much more certainty. Blanca de los Ríos seems to have been one of the first to realize that if, instead of searching merely for the elusive traces of the dramatist Tirso de Molina, one also looked for records of Gabriel Téllez the monk, then some information was available. She was able, with a certain amount of help, to locate a number of references to Fray Gabriel in Mercedarian and other archives, and thus to construct at least the skeleton of a biography, which she published in the introductions to her three-volume edition of Tirso's plays already referred to. Unfortunately the presentation is unsystematic, and the bare bones are fleshed with too much conjectural material no better substantiated than her theory of Tirso's origins. Her pioneer work therefore needed rectification and completion; but this has now been admirably achieved by Father Penedo. From such details as the records of Fray Gabriel's attendance at provincial and general chapters of his order; his signature among those of other monks on the occasion of some enactment; his name figuring in household accounts of expenditure on footwear and clothing; and from his own *Historia de la Merced* (*History of the Mercedarian Order*), which for so long lay unpublished and unread, Penedo has built up a chronology of the life of the dramatist-monk far more complete than the academicians of 1885 would ever have thought possible. It occupies the greater part of the three-hundred-page introduction to Volume I of Penedo's edition of the *History*, and the account that now follows is very largely taken from it.

Gabriel Téllez (he had not yet acquired his literary pseudonym) entered the Madrid house of the Mercedarian order as a novice in 1600, and was professed on 21 January 1601 in Guadalajara. The order of Our Lady of Mercy was a Catalan foundation, dating from the thirteenth century. Its original work had been the redemption of prisoners taken captive by the Moors, but after the Reconquest this gave way to preaching and general missionary activity throughout Spain, and also in Latin America where the order was one of the chief religious agencies at work. Its house in Guadalajara, where Gabriel made his profession, must have been an important one to judge from the number of provincial and even general chapters that were held there during his lifetime.

Now that the date of his profession and the probable year of his birth are known, it has become clear that he entered the cloister at the normal age of about nineteen, and not, as had been conjectured, after a long experience of the world. There then followed a protracted period of study: an arts course in Salamanca from 1601 to 1603, followed by theology in Toledo and Guadalajara from 1603 to 1607, and probably a further two years of theology in Alcalá de Henares. His presence is attested briefly in Soria in 1608, in Segovia in 1610, and in Madrid in 1610–1611, at which latter date he entered on a more settled period of some five years in Toledo.

VI His Early Dramatic Career

By now, his studies completed, he is beginning to write for the theater. His statement in the 1624 preliminaries to *The Country Houses of Toledo* that his plays have been gracing the stages for fourteen years, places the earliest of them in 1610, but it is not known which one this is. The first work that can be approximately dated is *El vergonzoso en palacio* (*The Shy Man at Court*), which must have been in existence by 1611: the text of this play, set in the late Middle Ages, includes a letter which in the manuscripts is anachronistically dated 15 July 1611, this presumably being the day on which either Tirso himself or an early copyist was at work. In a document of 1612 the manager of an acting company acknowledges the debt owed to "Padre Fray Gabriel Téllez" for the purchase of three plays in Toledo, indicating that the Mercedarian's dramatic career was by this time well established; and a number of plays can be shown to date from the two or three years that followed.

It seems strange that a young man living in a monastery, and in good standing with his community, was able to contract with theatrical managers and write plays for the public stage; especially as there already existed an active movement for the suppression of the theaters in the name of morality. Some of Tirso's works from this Toledan period are dramatized lives of saints, but others are frivolous comedies. *El vergonzoso en palacio* (*The Shy Man at Court*), *Don Gil de las calzas verdes* (*Don Gil of the Green Breeches*), and *Marta la piadosa* (*Pious Martha*), for instance, all depict heroines whose behavior is not of the most seemly, and whose roles seem to have been conceived, if not with particular actresses in mind, at least with a full awareness of what a good actress could achieve. A few years later, in *The Country Houses of Toledo*, Tirso was to attribute the failure of *Don Gil* on the Toledo stage to the unsuitability of the fat and aging actress who played the leading part. It would be interesting to know how close a contact he was able to have with the theatrical world. The time would come when he and other theater-going priests would be reproved for it; but for the moment nothing seems to have prevented his simultaneous pursuit of two such apparently incongruous careers.

Perhaps he was accorded special privileges because of the favor of his influential friends. This was the time when he was frequenting the houses of the Toledan aristocracy, in particular, it seems, the mansion of Buenavista, home of the Cardinal Archbishop Don Bernardo de Sandoval y Rojas. With a patron of such eminence, lesser authorities were perhaps unlikely to call his behavior in question. And if he was on friendly terms with the head of the Spanish church he must also have been close to the chief political power, for Sandoval's nephew was the duke of Lerma, minister of Philip III and the effective ruler of the country during the latter part of that king's reign. Professor Wade has drawn attention to a letter of Lope de Vega, dating from 1615 or early 1616, which seems to refer to Tirso and his intimacy with Lerma: "Don Molina is so well in with the Dukes of the divine hierarchy that he no longer remembers me."[14]

Tirso's Life

(Wade had previously shown that Téllez had begun to use the pseudonym Tirso de Molina at any rate by 1616.)[15] Does the ironical "Don Molina" imply that Lope regarded Tirso as a parvenu who had no more right than he himself to the title of "Don"?

VII *In the West Indies*

This first and very successful phase of Tirso's career came to an end when he was selected by his order to join a mission to its province of Santo Domingo on the island of Hispaniola (the present-day Dominican Republic), which was greatly in need of reform. The selection was obviously a mark of his superiors' regard, yet one wonders if at the same time they saw it as a means of weaning him from the distractions, both social and theatrical, of Toledo. The party of six monks sailed from Seville at the end of June 1616. Reference has already been made to the document authorizing their voyage which gives Fray Gabriel's age, rightly or wrongly, as thirty-three. He is described in it as preacher and lecturer, and also as being dark and with a high forehead.

He himself later gave in his *History of the Mercedarian Order* some idea of the work of his team in Santo Domingo. Though he was "the one who achieved least and was of least use," his companions "from the moment they set foot in the convent so restored losses and remedied neglect, that through sermons, lectures, and indefatigable exhortations they transformed not merely that house but also the others of their obedience into a community of exemplary men, a school of learned monks, a commerce of spiritual interests and a semblance of paradise" (II, 357). The doctrine of the Immaculate Conception, hitherto almost unknown in the island, was actively propagated, and the local members of the order were taught theology so efficiently that the province soon became self-sufficient in this respect, without further need of help from Spain.

Téllez himself delivered three lecture courses in theology of six months each. Despite his modest disclaimer, his successful performance of his duties is attested by his appointment as *Definidor*, or member of the governing body of the province. An opportunity for literary activity came when a poetic competition was held to celebrate the election of Our Lady of Mercy as the patron saint of Santo Domingo. Téllez submitted a number of poems (later published in his miscellany *Deleitar aprovechando [Pleasure with Profit]*), all of which won prizes. Plays were also performed on this occasion, but it is not known if any were his. None of his extant dramatic works appear to date from this two-year stay in the West Indies.

More surprising than this apparent intermission is the fact that when he does return to Spain and to the theater he draws very little on his Caribbean experiences.[16] A modern writer would no doubt look on foreign travel of this kind as an enrichment and an opportunity to acquire new and original material; one senses that Tirso felt it rather as an exile from the world of letters. There is a parallel here with his contemporary Juan Ruiz de Alarcón, who, although himself a Mexican, preferred to set his plays in Spain rather than in the New World. This must have been partly the effect of living in an age less individualistic than our own, which did not prize originality or approve departures from the norm; and partly because it was in Spain that all the excitement and growing intellectual ferment were then to be found.

VIII His Heyday in Madrid

Téllez was recalled to Spain for the general chapter of the order held at Guadalajara in June 1618. He then renounced the office of *Definidor* in the province of Santo Domingo and undertook two further years of lecturing, this time in Segovia, in order to earn the title of *Presentado* (a qualification as teacher of theology) in the province of Castile. At the same time he must have renewed contact with the Toledan friends about whom he writes in *The Country Houses of Toledo* (prepared for the press in 1621), and with the public theaters. In 1620 or 1621 came the move for which he must have been longing: transfer to the house of his order in Madrid. Madrid was the center of theatrical life, and there above all he would find it easy to pursue his twin vocations.

The cultural climate of Madrid at this time must have been powerfully stimulating. Among its inhabitants in the early 1620s were at least five men recognized today as major figures in the history of European literature: Góngora, Quevedo, Lope de Vega, and Calderón, as well as Tirso himself. Others, scarcely less eminent in Spanish letters, had been drawn in by the magnet of the theatergoing public and its insatiable demand for new plays: Guillén de Castro from Valencia, Vélez de Guevara and Mira de Amescua from Andalusia, and Ruiz de Alarcón from across the Atlantic. Tirso entered into all the excitement of their literary world, frequenting academies, taking sides in controversies, competing in poetic contests, and above all writing for the stage. Now in this ample setting he could spread his wings, those wings of native talent and hard work that were to carry him to the heights. These years constitute the second and more important phase of his dramatic career. He had "arrived," in the city itself and in the estimation of its populace; this was his heyday.

Yet his situation was not entirely as he might have wished. There had been a change of regime in Spain. Philip III, a king whom he had loved and respected, died on 31 March 1621. Lerma had fallen from power, and with him his entourage among whom Tirso had moved in Toledo. The sixteen-year-old Philip IV now occupied the throne, and government was in the hands of his favorite and chief minister, the count-duke of Olivares. Recent assessments of Olivares reveal him as a politician of some acumen, who might have done something to arrest the frightening economic decline of Spain if he had had any support from the privileged classes.[17] But in his day he was widely hated, for his ascendancy over the king and his own assumption of power as much as for the unpopular fiscal measures he was obliged to take. Tirso shared in this hatred, in his case perhaps intensified by his loyalty to his friends of the earlier regime. In more than one play of this period he attacks the institution of *privado,* or royal favorite, and even on occasion paints satirical portraits of Olivares himself.

IX *The Edict of 1625*

It was not to be expected that he could continue on this course with impunity. The blow fell on 6 March 1625, when a resolution of the Committee for Reform of the Council of Castile declared: "The meeting considered the scandal caused by a Mercedarian friar named Maestro Téllez, otherwise known as Tirso, by his writing of profane plays which set a bad example. And since the affair is notorious, it was agreed to petition His Majesty that the confessor should tell the nuncio to expel him hence to one of the more remote monasteries of his order, and forbid him on pain of excommunication to write plays or any other kind of profane verse. This to be done immediately."

At first sight this prohibition seems to be no more than the natural consequence of the anomaly already noted, that a man of the cloth should compose works which at best might be thought frivolous, at worst immoral. There had for some years been a strong movement for moral reform in the country, and the committee set up to consider this had more than once turned its attention to the dangerous influence of the theater. Yet why should Tirso, out of the many poet-priests of the period, have been selected for special condemnation? It seems clear that he had fallen foul of Olivares in some more personal manner than the rest.

Other elements in the affair are hinted at by Tirso in his play *Antona García*.[18] In a scene clearly inserted after March 1625 he presents himself as fleeing from Madrid, on account of envious enemies who have denounced him for providing recreation for others. He plays on the theme of envy, as in the regatta scene of *The Country Houses of Toledo*, and suggests that personal rivalries are involved. One of the objects of his resentment is a famous and outstanding poet, who can only be Lope de Vega; another is a man much less talented than Tirso himself who has nevertheless worked to have him condemned. Who can this have been, and what is the connection of these personal and literary quarrels with Olivares and the movement for reform?

Two different answers to these questions have lately been proposed. Father Penedo suggests that the enemy was a fellow Mercedarián, Fray Pedro Franco de Guzmán; he was a relative of Olivares, and having sensed satire against himself in Tirso's plays, retaliated by getting his powerful kinsman to take action against their author. Professor Kennedy, on the other hand, sets the controversy wholly within the literary circles close to the court, and identifies the unnamed detractor as the court poet Antonio Hurtado de Mendoza. Mendoza enjoyed the favor of Olivares, who was an Andalusian like himself; and he would certainly have been in a position to destroy any enemy if he felt inclined to do so.[19]

Professor Kennedy's conclusions are supported by a great deal of circumstantial evidence, and seem to offer the more convincing explanation of the affair. The whole of her *Studies in Tirso, I* is an impressive reconstruction of Tirso's activity on the literary scene of the 1620s, with its satires, rivalries, and feuds. She often has to rely on probabilities in default of conclusive evidence, and on her own reading of obscure allusions that might perhaps admit of other interpretations; but her profound knowledge of the period and its writings inspires considerable confidence in her reconstruction of the events.

X Later Years as a Mercedarian

The resolution of the Committee for Reform virtually ended Tirso's dramatic career. It does not appear to have been implemented to the letter, since a handful of plays can be assigned to later years, but his close association with the theaters of the capital had come to an end. The next month, April 1625, finds him in Seville, and though he is back in Madrid the following year, it seems to have been only while awaiting the decision of his order as to which of its remote monasteries should now receive him. The chapter met at Guadalajara in May 1626, and posted him to Trujillo in the southwest; but in the responsible position of *Comendador*.

Téllez was evidently not out of favor with his superiors, which again makes it seem likely that the real reasons for his silencing were not moral. There was in any case no love lost between Olivares and the Mercedarians, and they probably resented any interference by the civil authorities in the affairs of one of their own number. If there was little future for Tirso the dramatist, there was still a home and a sphere of activity for Gabriel Téllez the monk; and the story of his life from 1626 is very largely that of his Mercedarian career.

He spent three years in the wilderness in Trujillo, after which the election of his friend and former teacher, Fray Pedro Merino, as head of the Castilian province, enabled him to be brought back nearer the capital. In 1629 the order was celebrating the canonization of its founder San Pedro Nolasco, and Tirso organized a literary competition in Salamanca in honor of the event. Penedo suggests plausibly that it may have been the religious fervor generated at this time that led Tirso to pen an Act of Contrition. The existence of this has long been known, but the text has only recently been located by Penedo in a late seventeenth-century publication, and reproduced by him as an appendix to Tirso's *History of the Mercedarian Order* (II, 647–51). It takes the form of a long poem full of very generalized expressions of penitence and devotion.

Tirso also gave an earnest of his changed outlook in his next major work, *Deleitar aprovechando (Pleasure with Profit)*, written in 1631–1632 and published in 1635. This is an exact counterpart of *The Country Houses of Toledo:* a framed miscellany in which a group of lords and ladies meet to entertain each other with a variety of diversions including the telling of stories and the performing of plays. But whereas the content of *The Country Houses* was wholly secular, this time the stories are lives of saints and the plays are *autos sacramentales*, one-act allegorical pieces for the feast of Corpus Christi.

In 1632 Téllez's standing in the order was confirmed by his appointment as its chronicler. This post had been held by Fray Alonso Remón, who had left a history of the order half written. Tirso's commission was to complete this, and he again settled in Madrid in order to do so. It is probably not a mere coincidence that during this period of residence in Madrid four volumes of his collected plays emerged from the press (a first volume having appeared in 1627). It seems clear that Tirso was once again in some measure of contact with the literary circles of the capital, and that although he was forbidden, and indeed now unwilling, to write plays for the public theaters, he had not entirely lost interest in his earlier work.

By 1636 he had brought Remón's chronicle up to date, but then apparently took the sudden decision to scrap Remón's work and rewrite the whole of the first part himself. This task took him a further three years; but the *History of the Mercedarian Order* as completed in 1639 was wholly his. It was a great achievement, and his last major work. In it he announced plans for further undertakings in his capacity as chronicler of the order: lives of some of its illustrious members, histories of its convents, a study of the various miraculous statues of Our Lady of Mercy. But the only work of this nature to have been begun, as far as is known, was his *Life of Santa María de Cervellón*, of which a fragment survives.[20] That his pen was still active in other directions is shown by the events that followed.

In 1640 the house of the order in Madrid received a visitation from Fray Marcos Salmerón, the vicar provincial. He deposed Tirso from the office of chronicler, dismissed him to the monastery of Cuenca, and issued an edict forbidding any of the Mercedarians of Madrid to write satires in verse or prose against the government. This edict suggests that Tirso was being censured on political grounds. Olivares was by now more hated than ever, and the Mercedarian order, with its Catalan origins, resented his antiseparatist policies which had led to a rebellion in Catalonia. Tirso had made plain his Catalan sympathies in *Pleasure with Profit*, and it would not be surprising if he had also expressed himself in political satires which had somehow come to the notice of authority.

If this was the explanation, Tirso paid dearly for his daring. A second time he was banished to the wilderness; a second eminent career was in ruins. He protested to Salmerón, but in vain. And when the latter became general of the order in 1642, another blow fell: he rejected Tirso's great *History* and relegated it to the archives, where it remained, unpublished and almost unread, for over three hundred years.

The next year, ironically, Olivares himself fell from power; but this brought only limited relief for Tirso. He was allowed to move from cold, remote Cuenca to Toledo, and in 1645 he received his last appointment, that of *Comendador* in the convent of Soria, another outlying city of the Castilian province. He was long thought to have died there, but Penedo has shown that his death took place some little distance away, in Almazán. A requiem was said for him in Segovia on 24 February 1648, so that, allowing time for the news to travel, it may be assumed that he had died about 20 February of that year.

It had been a strange seesaw of a life, with two distinct, and distinguished, careers, and three separate periods of literary achievement, each brought suddenly to a close: the first by the call to Santo Domingo, the other two by silencing and exile. Tirso's work as a dramatist was virtually completed by the time he was forty-five, and the last third of his lifetime was spent largely in other pursuits; but that work had already won for him, as he had announced it would, the laurel wreath of everlasting fame.

CHAPTER 2

Tirso's Theater

WHEN Tirso began to write, the modern theater as a commercial form of public entertainment was not very old. Such Spanish drama as had existed a hundred years earlier was in the form of simple one-act pieces, performed either in or near the church or in the private households of the aristocracy. The theater as an institution was the creation of the Renaissance; and the Italian influences that encouraged its development tended in two different directions. Via Italian commentaries on Aristotle's *Poetics* came an interest in classical drama following the pattern of the ancient Greek tragedians and Seneca; while writers like Ariosto and Machiavelli, imitating in their own comedies the Latin works of Plautus and Terence, helped to popularize a livelier, more sensational drama full of action and intrigue.

There was little doubt which mode would prove commercially more successful. Aristotelian drama as developed by Corneille would eventually make its appeal to cultured middle-class audiences in France; in Spain it had its handful of practitioners, and its supporters who became increasingly shrill as their cause was seen to be lost. But the plays the audiences flocked to see were those of the livelier type, popularized above all by Lope de Vega. It was Lope who proved able to fuse together ingredients from the Italianate drama of intrigue and national elements from the early history, legend, and literature of Spain, in such a way as to produce a new dramatic form, one which was to occupy the theaters of Spain for little short of a century. It was well established by the time Tirso began his dramatic career, and it provided the mold in which all his plays were cast.

I   *The Lopean Drama*

The Lopean type of play has three acts and is written in verse. It uses a variety of meters, with short, octosyllabic lines predominating. It does not observe the classical unities of time and place, and though it may have one single action there are more often at least two, with main plot and subplot interwoven. Action is swift and sensational: duels and murders, abduction and rape are not uncommon, and the intrigue arising from concealments, feigned identities, and obfuscation of various kinds is very common indeed. The schemes of lovers to overcome rivals or outwit stern fathers are a frequent mainspring of action; so is the strict code of gentlemanly honor, which requires a noble to avenge by the sword any lowering of his esteem in the eyes of others, and imposes rigid standards of behavior on women.

Whether the main action is serious or comic there is always some light relief, usually provided by the *gracioso*, or comic actor, who was to be found in every acting company and has a part in virtually every play. Other recurrent stock types are the maidservant, the elderly father, and the two or three pairs of lovers. A theater of such pace as Lope's does not offer scope for great depth of characterization, and although both Lope and Tirso certainly did create memorable figures, characters generally reveal themselves in action much more than through soliloquy or introspection. Similarly with language: the dialogue usually moves too fast to allow for much poetic elaboration, and the Golden Age theater is not on the whole a theater of great poetry; even though the action may be deliberately held up at times for the singing of a song, or the recitation of a poetic set-piece in the form of ballad, sonnet or gloss.

Within the obvious artificiality of its verse, language on the whole (at least up to the time of Calderón) approximates to that of normal speech; and this blend of realism with convention in the diction is matched by the way in which the sensational foreground action is so often set against a convincing backcloth of everyday life. Mention is made of familiar details like the streets and churches of Madrid, local festivals, or the tasks and produce of the countryside, in a deliberate attempt to suspend the audience's disbelief and win its acceptance of the unlikely stories.

The Lopean drama, though it began as popular entertainment, did eventually prove itself capable of treating deeper issues and becoming the mouthpiece of both moral teaching and metaphysical exploration. But this was a late development, before which it had to be tried and purified in the fire of heated controversy.

II Tirso and the Controversy

Lope's theater was attacked on two scores. Firstly it shocked the Aristotelians because in their eyes it debased a noble art form cultivated by the great dramatists of Greece and Rome. Literary composition of any kind was an art, a craft, which had its accepted rules and norms; but Lope ignored these, and in his bid for popularity produced works which a refined literary taste could only see as monstrosities. Secondly the theater attracted censure as a danger to morality. Audiences often behaved in an unseemly way, and were further provoked by the actresses' display of themselves, particularly when dressed in male attire as the plays often required them to be. While the Aristotelians therefore campaigned for a drama that would conform to the rules, there was a strong movement among the moralists for the theaters to be closed altogether.

Lope came into open conflict with his two groups of attackers at about the time when Tirso was beginning to write. In 1609 the historian Mariana published a *Treatise against Public Entertainments*, which Lope answered with his *New Art of Writing Plays*. This is a jocular piece in verse, in which he admits his disregard for the classical rules and his acceptance of the criterion of popular appeal; but also goes on to claim status for himself as the creator of a new kind of art, different from but not necessarily inferior to that of the ancients.

It might have been expected that Tirso, as a churchman and a friend of aristocratic patrons, would join the antipopular party; yet from the start his plays follow the pattern established by Lope. In fact in the first major phase of his production he makes no reference to the existence of any controversy; but after his return from Santo Domingo, by which time Lope had suffered further bitter attacks, he comes out boldly and exuberantly in defense of his master.

Tirso's main contributions to the debate are to be found in three separate passages of *The Country Houses of Toledo*, a work that was being put together in 1620–1621. Among the festivities he describes there one took the form of a performance of his own play *El vergonzoso en palacio* (*The Shy Man at Court*), already by that time some nine years old. One of its heroines, Serafina, is stagestruck; and Tirso makes her the mouthpiece for an apologia for the Lopean drama, almost certainly inserted into her role at this later date.[1] Her cousin Juana questions whether it is proper for a young lady to act, particularly in male costume; but Serafina lists the many kinds of pleasure that a play can give, and the various ways in which the theater has been described, including the Ciceronian "image of life." It is, she says, a banquet that leaves fools hungry but satisfies the wise; and she ends with a challenge: "Which of these two parties do you wish to belong to?" Her hearers would undoubtedly identify these two parties, the fools and the wise, with those involved in the current controversy.

After the performance of the play the assembled gentry discuss it. One member of the group criticizes the dramatist for tampering with history, another expresses a strongly Aristotelian and conservative view of what the drama should be. A third, Tirso's mouthpiece on this occasion, answers by distinguishing, in scholastic terms, between the "substance" of drama, which will always be the same, and the "accidents" which, without any disrespect to the classics, may legitimately be changed with the passage of time. Moreover, if the ancient world had its Aeschylus and Euripides, its Seneca and Terence, modern Spain has its Lope de Vega, who has already done enough to constitute a school in himself, and to win the firm support of all those proud to call themselves his disciples. Thus Tirso declares his allegiance to his master, and reasserts with more assurance the claim tentatively made by Lope himself to have created a new genre, as respectable and praiseworthy as the old.

The final entertainment in *The Country Houses* is another of Tirso's own plays, *El celoso prudente* (*Jealous but Prudent*). Again a discussion follows, and this time it is the moralists against whom the author defends himself: "Now let the critics sharpen their complaints on the stone of envy! Let us see if those hairsplitters can find here anything worthy of reproof! Let the Catos censor this entertainment, for however closely they examine it, modest habits will find in it no occasion of distraction. . . . All those present can learn from it to esteem the modern theater which in these days, purged of the imperfections that formerly marred the Spanish stage and free from all lewd action, delights while teaching and teaches in giving pleasure" (II, 256–57). With this enunciation of the Horatian principle of pleasure with profit, Tirso cleverly enlists the classics on his own side.

It is noteworthy that he admits that there has been an improvement. Before Lope's opponents are too hastily condemned for their narrow-mindedness it should be remembered, firstly that their attitude was only that which educated upholders of aesthetic values in any age are prone to adopt toward the "pop art" of their day; and secondly, that their criticisms did have a beneficial effect. The controversy resulted in a raising of standards, aesthetic as well as moral, and it is possible that without it neither Lope nor Tirso would have attained the heights they did. The purgation they were induced to apply both strengthened their own drama and brought the Golden Age theater to a state in which their successor Calderón could take it over as a positive instrument of reform, thus ensuring its survival for a further generation.

III Problems of Publication

Both Lope and Tirso at the beginning of their careers thought of themselves as ephemeral entertainers and took no steps to preserve their plays. Only at a fairly late stage, when his reputation was beginning to be threatened by false attributions and the circulation of mangled texts, did Lope realize the advantages of collecting and publishing his own dramatic works. Volumes, or *partes*, of his collected plays were being brought out by others from 1604 onward, but *Parte* IX which appeared in 1617 was the first one to be supervised by Lope himself. Tirso seems not to have thought of publication during the first phase of his career, and sent no plays to the press before the three included in *The Country Houses of Toledo*. His five *partes* were published only after he had virtually stopped writing for the theater.

The process of collection was not an easy one. The original manuscript of each play had been sold to the manager of an acting company, whose property it then became. He rehearsed it, put it on for a brief run, and then probably discarded it, after which it survived, if at all, only in the copies made for the cast. But these might well have been cut or otherwise altered in rehearsal, since the author retained no rights in his own text. Many plays were thus irretrievably lost, and very few survived in their original form. Nevertheless the publication by a dramatist of his own work does offer a reasonable guarantee that the text as it appears in print was at least acceptable to him.

When a play was published by someone other than its author, either singly or in a collection of some dozen or so works by different dramatists, no such guarantee exists. The text might be based on an actor's copy containing unauthorized alterations. Or it might have been acquired in a more underhand way, by employing a professional memorizer to attend a performance and then write down what he could remember; this practice led to the circulation of some highly corrupt versions. Plays were also often wrongly attributed, by accident or design. In some cases it had genuinely been forgotten who was the author of a work first staged many years before. In others the ascription of an inferior piece to, say, Lope de Vega might draw in the audiences or help to sell a volume, and conversely the misappropriation of a work genuinely by Lope might boost the reputation of a struggling dramatist. Uncertainty also arose when a play was revived after an interval and, as often happened, reworked by a later hand.

For all these reasons the Spanish Golden Age theater has come down to us fraught with textual inaccuracies, doubtful attributions, and obscurities of many kinds; and the theater of Tirso de Molina offers some particularly teasing problems.

IV *Publication of Tirso's Plays: the First* Parte

In *The Country Houses of Toledo* Tirso announced his intention of publishing his plays in *partes,* and declared that he already had a first *parte* of twelve plays in the press (I, 13). The prologue containing this statement was probably written not at the time the book received its censors' approval in 1621, but in 1624, the actual year of publication. Even so the First *parte* did not appear until 1627, and then not in Madrid, where Tirso had published *The Country Houses,* but in Seville. Why the long delay and the new place of publication? And why did this Seville edition lack the necessary license and other preliminaries, although these were all present, dated Madrid, 1626, in a reissue of the collection dated Valencia, 1631?

Of the various explanations suggested in recent years it is that of Jaime Moll which seems to get to the root of the matter. The Committee for Reform at its meeting on 6 March 1625 did not only proceed against Tirso: it also recommended that the Council of Castile should grant no more licenses for the publication of novels or plays; and Moll brings out the striking fact that the Council did indeed grant no such licenses between 1625 and 1634. This explains the ten-year gap between the appearance of Lope's *Partes* XX and XXI, and much of the resentment over false attributions by authors who were unable to get their own works out during this period.

The prohibition did not extend to the kingdom of Aragon, and so it was still possible to publish in such cities as Barcelona and Valencia. Seville did come under the ban, and the flourishing book trade there responded with clandestine editions and other ruses, such as false preliminaries to make it appear that a work had been published in Aragon. These practices were specifically forbidden when the ban became law on 13 June 1627, but they continued nevertheless, with the result that ostensible dates and places of publication during this period cannot always be taken at their face value.[2]

In the case of Tirso's First *parte*, Moll shows that a license for this was granted on 11 June 1624, thus bearing out Tirso's statement in the prologue to *The Country Houses;* but printing evidently did not proceed fast enough for it to beat the clampdown of the following year. Baulked of publishing in Madrid, Tirso probably took his manuscript with him to Seville in 1625 and had it brought out there without a license. When vigilance was reinforced after the decree of 1627 the volume was reissued with false preliminaries and place of publication, to make it appear that it had come out legally in Aragon.[3] Moll's simple explanation follows naturally from his important discovery about the full effects of the 1625 recommendation.

V *The Third* Parte

It was a long time before Tirso published any more plays. Prefacing his next *parte* in 1634 he, or his nephew, declares that for ten years he has resisted all persuasions to issue any more, having learned his lesson from the tricks played on him in the past. But it is clear that the climate is beginning to change, for after this collection a book of short stories is promised, and also a second volume of *The Country Houses of Toledo*. (In fact neither of these ever appeared.)[4]

The new *parte*, like its predecessor, has its puzzling features. The fact that it was published in distant Tortosa, although Tirso was then living in Madrid, is explained by the prohibition still in force in Castile. But why was it called the Third *parte?* There was as yet no second, and it is quite plain from the preface that this was the first volume to break the long silence. A new edition of *The Country Houses*, with three plays included as before, had appeared in Barcelona in 1631, and the printers may perhaps have thought of this as a second *parte;* or they may simply have made a mistake.

Curiosity is also aroused by the first appearance of Tirso's nephew, Francisco Lucas de Avila, as collector and editor of the plays. Francisco's preface and dedication are of considerable interest. He is at great pains to distinguish his role from that of his uncle. Tirso has been hurt by his past experiences and wants to have nothing more to do with profane literature; Francisco has abstracted, nay stolen, his old manuscripts from him, and is publishing them on his own responsibility, without his uncle's knowledge and doubtless to his great annoyance; even the forthcoming prose collections are to be based on old forgotten notebooks of the uncle, now edited and supplemented by the nephew.

It might be thought very likely that Tirso's change of course about 1630, his Act of Contrition and his new eminence in his order, would indeed dissuade him from publishing more plays, and that Francisco's preface should be taken at its face value; Penedo certainly thinks so. But many critics have pointed out that Francisco writes in a style indistinguishable from the inflated, contrived manner adopted by Tirso himself in his prose works, even to the extent of using some of the same images and turns of phrase. It also seems significant that the subsequent Second, Fourth, and Fifth *partes* are likewise said to have been compiled by Francisco Lucas de Avila, but contain prefaces either explicitly by Tirso himself or, what amounts to the same thing, whimsically put into the mouth of his book. The truth seems to be that Francisco did exist and may have helped Tirso to get his plays into print, but in the preface to the Third *parte* was no more than his uncle's mouthpiece. The apparent disclaimer of personal responsibility would be a very natural device for Tirso to adopt if he wished to test the freer atmosphere of the 1630s without committing himself too far.

VI *The Second* Parte

The enigmas of the First and Third *partes* are minor compared with that presented by *Parte* II. This volume appeared in Madrid in 1635, the granting of licenses by then having been resumed. Francisco Lucas de Avila is said to have compiled it, but Tirso writes his own dedication, to the Madrid guild of booksellers which was bearing his printing costs. Of the twelve plays in the volume he dedicates "four which are mine in my own name, and in that of the owners of the other eight (which being children of such illustrious fathers, by I know not what misfortune of theirs have come to be laid at my door) those which remain."

How did it come about that one of an author's *partes*, licensed in his name and bearing his dedication, contained works by other men? Various explanations have been offered: that Tirso wrote all the plays himself and is making an ironical protest against the false claims that have been made to them; or that he had a hand in all twelve, but in eight of them collaborated with another author. Both these theories must be discarded now that it is established that three of the works are in fact by other dramatists: *La reina de los reyes* (*Queen of Kings*) by Hipólito de Vergara, and a pair of plays on Alvaro de Luna (two of the finest in the collection) by Mira de Amescua. Penedo thinks that this Second *parte* was a homage volume which Tirso's nephew and friends put together in order to honor him, including in it works of their own as well as his.[5] Professor Kennedy believes that Tirso compiled the volume himself, but intentionally included some plays by fellow dramatists.[6] Both these scholars presumably then see the failure to identify the "children of other fathers" as a simple omission on the part of the printers.

The Second *parte* is unlike the others in that it contains not only the usual twelve plays, but also a handful of poems and twelve *entremeses*, or one-act sketches, some of which are certainly by Quiñones de Benavente, the master of that genre. In this respect it resembles some of the early *partes* of Lope de Vega, known as *extravagantes*, which were published without his authority and included plays by others as well as himself. Yet Tirso obviously intervened to some extent in his own Second *parte*. It seems that there must have been something less than complete understanding between him and his printers, but the precise facts are difficult to determine.

Whatever the explanation, Tirso made some attempt to put the matter right in his dedication; but generations of scholars have wished that he could have been a little more explicit, and said plainly which were the four plays by him. For of all the uncertainties that still obscure the life and work of Tirso de Molina the most tantalizing is that of the authenticity of the plays in the Second *parte*. Two which mention his name in the closing lines are universally recognized as his: these are *Por el sótano y el torno* (*Through Basement and Hatch*) and *Amor y celos hacen discretos* (*Love and Jealousy Make Men Wise*). Thereafter one is reduced to arguing on the basis of similarities. *Esto sí que es negociar* (*That's Business!*) is another version of a play in the First *parte*, *El melancólico* (*The Melancholic*), and so has been generally accepted as the third of the four.[7] Candidates for the fourth place include *La mujer por fuerza* (*A Woman Against her Will*), suggested by Cotarelo because of its likeness to many of Tirso's comedies of intrigue, and in particular to *El amor médico* (*Love Turned Doctor*);[8] *Cautela contra cautela* (*Cunning Matched with Cunning*), strongly urged by Professor Kennedy on the basis of the material it has in common with other Tirsian works, notably *El amor y el amistad* (*Love and Friendship*);[9] and *El condenado por desconfiado* (*The Man of Little Faith*), which many critics have seen as a companion piece to the other great theological drama, *El burlador de Sevilla* (*The Trickster of Seville*).

El condenado por desconfiado (*The Man of Little Faith*) is an outstanding play, and for this reason too it has been thought that it must be the last of the four, since only one of the giants of the theater could have conceived it. There are, however, strong arguments for ascribing it to Mira de Amescua, a dramatist who has been considerably underrated in the past. The question of its authorship will be examined more fully when the play itself is analyzed in a later chapter. Meanwhile one can only register frustration at yet another Tirsian conundrum, and one that leaves the authorship of a masterpiece in doubt.

VII *The Fourth and Fifth* Partes

The remaining *partes* fortunately present no new problems. They were published in Madrid in 1635 and 1636 respectively. The copyright of Part IV was granted to Tirso, that of Part V to Francisco Lucas de Avila. Both bear the name of Francisco as compiler, but in each case the dedication is by Tirso, and the prologue is put into the mouth of the book itself. From *The Country Houses of Toledo* onward Tirso had been fond of the fancy of calling his works his children, and letting them speak in his name. This metaphor, which probably came naturally to a celibate writer, was again employed in each of these last two prefaces; and that to Part V announces that "señora madre" (presumably the printing press) is already pregnant with a sixth *parte*. Whether this really was so, and if so what happened to it, is not known; certainly no more Tirsian *partes* appeared.

In both Part IV and Part V Tirso is still presenting himself as the object of envy. Perhaps the personal animosities were still too strong for him; perhaps the published plays were not received as well as he had hoped. It seems likely that the cessation of the series was connected, as either cause or result, with his sudden decision to rewrite Remón's history of the order. At all events this task absorbed him for the next three years, and the year 1636 seems to mark his final adieu to the drama.

VIII The Canon and Number of Tirso's Plays

The Fifth *parte* contains only eleven plays instead of the usual twelve. There is no doubt, however, about what the missing one should have been: the last two plays in the volume are Parts I and II of *Santa Juana*, and there exists a manuscript in Tirso's own hand of the third part of this same trilogy. If we add together the thirty-six plays contained in *Partes* I, III, and IV, the eleven of *Parte* V with the *Santa Juana* manuscript making twelve, the three published in *The Country Houses*, and the three of *Parte* II which are known to be by Tirso, we arrive at a total of fifty-four plays which can safely be accepted as authentic. Eight other plays were attributed to Tirso in collections by various dramatists published during the seventeenth century, and a further nine either separately printed or surviving in manuscript also bore his name. Attributions of this kind are, as has been seen, often unreliable, and must be particularly suspect in the case of works first appearing some twenty or more years after their supposed author's death. Some of the seventeen doubtful plays will probably be by Tirso, others will not; and it lies outside the scope of this study to investigate the authorship of each one.

If to these seventeen we add the six from the Second *parte* whose paternity remains an open question, we have the texts of twenty-three plays that may or may not be by Tirso. Fortunately only two of these are of such interest or quality as to demand attention: *El condenado por desconfiado* (*The Man of Little Faith*), already mentioned, and *El burlador de Sevilla* (*The Trickster of Seville*), first published in a collection of 1630. Both these works, and their authorship, will be examined in a later chapter. For the rest Tirso's merit as a dramatist can be amply demonstrated by those plays that are known to be his, and it is from among these that the examples to be analyzed in this study will be chosen.

Even if all seventy-seven plays were authentic this would still be less than a fifth of what he claimed to have written. He referred in the preface to *The Country Houses* (1624) to an output of three hundred plays over fourteen years, and by the time of the prologue to the Third *parte* (1634) this has become more than four hundred plays over twenty years. That much of his work is lost there can be no doubt; yet the figures of three hundred and four hundred plays seem surprisingly high. Can they be taken literally?

Professor Kennedy has recently shown that it was not uncommon for dramatists to overstate their output.[10] Lope de Vega near the end of his life was speaking of his fifteen hundred plays, yet modern scholars estimate that he probably wrote no more than eight hundred. Tirso's claims too are probably exaggerated. An output of three hundred plays over fourteen years would mean an average of over twenty a year, or one every two and a half weeks. This seems a high rate to sustain, even making no allowance for time lost through other activities, such as the missionary work in the West Indies. It seems similarly unlikely that he could have added a further one hundred between 1624 and 1634. The figure of four hundred plays is therefore probably too high for his total production; but it is not unreasonable to think that this should still be measured in hundreds rather than in tens, and that his extant authenticated theater represents perhaps less than a quarter of what he actually wrote.

IX Dating

It is clear that the publication of Tirso's plays bears no relation to their date of composition, and that the chronology of his theater must be deduced from other data.

External evidence will sometimes provide a *terminus ad quem*. For instance, we know that a Toledan actor-manager contracted to buy *Cómo han de ser los amigos (True Friendship)*, *La elección por la virtud (Elected for his Virtue)*, and *Tanto es lo de más como lo de menos (Enough is as Good as a Feast)*[11] in September 1612; that Tirso himself wrote out the text of *Santa Juana*, Part I, in May 1613, and that of Part III of the same trilogy in August 1614;[12] and that *Don Gil de las calzas verdes (Don Gil of the Green Breeches)* was staged in Toledo in July 1615.[13] In each case the play concerned had probably been written only a short time beforehand.

A slightly vaguer indication of the date of a play is sometimes provided by the name of the actor-manager who first put it on. The first printing of *Amor y celos hacen discretos (Love and Jealousy Make Men Wise)*, in the Second *parte*, is headed with the statement that it was performed by Valdés in Seville; as it is known that Pedro de Valdés and his company were active in Seville in the years 1615–1617 the play can fairly safely be assigned to that period.

Similarly, Tirso himself states when including his *auto sacramental Los hermanos parecidos* (*The Identical Brothers*) in *Pleasure with Profit*, that its leading roles were first taken by the twins Juan Bautista and Juan Jerónimo Valenciano; this dates the *auto* before 17 February 1624, on which date Juan Bautista was murdered.

Internal evidence from the plays themselves is more plentiful, though not always conclusive. Where a source can be established this will sometimes furnish a *terminus a quo*. For example, for his *Santa Juana* plays Tirso undoubtedly used Antonio Daza's life of the saint, first published in 1611; and he himself acknowledges having based *Las Quinas de Portugal* (*The Arms of Portugal*) on the *Epítome de las historias portuguesas* of Faria y Sousa, which appeared in 1628. The death in 1619 of the much revered Jacopo Trenchi, known as the "Caballero de Gracia," must have been the occasion for Tirso's play of that title; and his trilogy on the Pizarro family[14] almost certainly arose from his presence in Trujillo, city of the Pizarros, in 1626–1629.

The subject matter of a play may in certain cases reflect some concern that was topical at the time of its composition. Professor Kennedy has shown how the backgrounds of some plays of the early 1620s—*La fingida Arcadia* (*Feigned Arcady*), *El celoso prudente* (*Jealous but Prudent*)—reveal an interest in distant parts of Europe then becoming known through the Thirty Years' War;[15] and also how *La prudencia en la mujer* (*Prudence in Woman*), *Privar contra su gusto* (*The Reluctant Favorite*), and others, in touching on the sensitive question of royal favorites, echo the growing disquiet about the influence of Olivares over the young Philip IV in the opening years of that king's reign.

Far more frequently it is some incidental allusion that offers a pointer. Mention has already been made of the letter dated 1611 in some manuscripts of *The Shy Man at Court*. *La villana de Vallecas* (*The Village Girl from Vallecas*) likewise contains a dated letter, this time written on 25 March 1620; and the date of 1620 is confirmed by a reference to Philip III, who died in March 1621 but is still alive at the time of writing. *Marta la piadosa* (*Pious Martha*) contains a long account, extraneous to the plot, of the Spanish capture of the Moorish fortress of La Mamora which took place on 6 August 1614; since such a narrative would only be of interest when topical, it may be assumed that the play was written, or had that speech inserted in it, shortly after that date.

A line of investigation that Professor Kennedy has made peculiarly her own concerns changes in fashion, and the sumptuary decrees passed in November 1622 in an attempt to curb extravagance in dress and other forms of display. By noting references to the new popularity of blue eyes or black hair, or to regulations against the use of coaches or the wearing of starched ruffs and point lace, she has been able to assign a large number of plays, or at least certain passages in those plays, to Tirso's prolific period in the 1620s.[16]

Incidental allusions can be misleading, however, in that they may have been inserted some time after the original composition; perhaps to add topicality when a play was being revived, or at a later stage still, when it was being prepared for publication. They are not therefore infallible instruments of dating. Professor Kennedy repeatedly has to say that a play was "written or reworked" in such-and-such a year; and she has occasionally found it necessary to revise some of her earlier suggestions. There is also a danger of seeing an allusion where none exists: of reading a topical or personal meaning into innocent words that are merely part of the fabric of the play. It is this tendency above all which vitiates the apparently impressive chronology constructed by Blanca de los Ríos, and elaborated in the introductions to her three volumes of Tirso's dramatic works. As with her biographical study, she deserves great credit for opening up important lines of investigation, but she too often allows them to lead her to unwarranted conclusions.

There remain at least two other tools that can be used to determine the period of a play's composition. Spanish Golden Age drama is written in a variety of metrical forms. Some meters were commoner at one time, some at another, according to fashion and the changing practice of individual dramatists. There does not exist for Tirso anything comparable to the invaluable *Chronology of Lope de Vega's Comedias* compiled by S. G. Morley and Courtney Bruerton on the basis of Lope's versification;[17] but Bruerton has shown that in Tirso too the percentages of the different meters used in a play may give some indication of its date.[18] Generally speaking, *redondillas* are an early meter, whose role as the backbone of the text was gradually taken over by *romance*. *Décimas* only became common in later years, as did the Italianate *silva*.

Any individual's use of words will also change over the years, and it is on the basis of the vocabulary used that André Nougué assigns *La venganza de Tamar* (*Tamar's Vengeance*) to the year 1623.[19]

Nougué promises to explain his reasons in a full study of Tirso's vocabulary, and it is clear that such a study may yield a considerable amount of useful chronological information. The later Golden Age theater as a whole tended to move away from the relatively natural diction employed by Lope toward more *culto* writing, that is, a learned, elevated, and ingenious poetic style that showed the influence of Góngora. Although Góngora's deliberate obscurity roused furious opposition, from Lope and Tirso among others, it also insinuated itself into the literary consciousness of the age, and much of the poetry and drama of the 1620s and 1630s, including Tirso's own, contains echoes of his style. Passages of *culto* writing in a Tirso play will nearly always indicate a later rather than an earlier work.

It is not possible to reproduce here all that is already known about the dates of Tirso's plays; for that reference must be made to the invaluable studies of Ruth Lee Kennedy, Courtney Bruerton, and Gerald E. Wade.[20] But neither is very much detailed information necessary for an understanding of Tirso's theater and its development. The great majority of his plays seem to have been written during a mere decade and a half, between about 1610 and 1625; and within that span it is possible to isolate two five-year periods of particularly intense activity, 1611–1616 and 1620–1625. If a play can be assigned with reasonable certainty to one or other of those short spells, that is for most purposes a sufficient indication of its place within his theater; and fortunately nearly all the plays examined in this study can be so assigned.

CHAPTER 3

Intrigue and Illusion

I *The Comedy of Intrigue*

IT was not merely in Spain that Italianate comedy flourished. The titles of two of Shakespeare's plays, *The Merchant of Venice* and *Two Gentlemen of Verona*, proclaim their Italian origin, as do the settings of *The Tempest, Much Ado About Nothing,* and *The Taming of the Shrew*. Other plays set in a variety of locations—Illyria, Bohemia, even the forest of Arden—derive ultimately from the same source. For the stuff of his plots Shakespeare relies to a surprising extent on dramatic formulae: rivalry between brothers, as in *The Tempest* or *As You Like It;* false reports of death, as in *Much Ado* or *The Winter's Tale;* girls masquerading as men, as in *As You Like It* and *Twelfth Night;* and, following from this, mistaken identity and the complete impenetrability of all disguise, so that women fall in love with women, and men in love with women cease to recognize them as soon as they don doublet and hose. These conventions are the legacy of Italian romance, whether in the form of play or short story; and Lope de Vega, Shakespeare's senior by two years, was also drawing on this legacy at the same time.

The Italian material came to Spain not only in book form, but also with the troupes of Italian players who toured the peninsula in the latter part of the sixteenth century, giving performances of the largely improvised *commedia dell'arte* type, and also probably of more literary pieces.[1] Valencia, on the Mediterranean seaboard, saw many of them, and under their influence had developed a thriving theater of its own by the time Lope de Vega arrived there, exiled from Madrid, in 1588. Lope probably learned from the Valencian theater at least as much as he gave to it; and the comedy of intrigue which he popularized as a result soon came to dominate the Spanish stage.[2]

There was therefore a flourishing genre for Tirso to turn his hand to, and he contributed some notable examples to it. Most of them follow a broadly similar pattern: there is a falling in love, but the love meets with obstacles—it is perhaps unrequited, or the beloved proves fickle, or there are jealous rivals, or the parents have other plans for their children; the lover then devises a stratagem involving pretence of some kind—disguise, impersonation, or some other misrepresentation of the facts; the ensuing complications rise to an hilarious climax, very often in a night scene in which darkness increases the confusion; the denouement comes with revelations and clarifications, and the young people are paired off—the principal couple satisfactorily, the others sometimes in a casual and perfunctory way which ignores their feelings and simply provides a neat rounding off. But within this overall pattern there are many differences of detail.

II El vergonzoso en palacio (The Shy Man at Court)

The Shy Man at Court is a play full of incident, with three separate actions, one centered on each of the three main characters. The first concerns Mireno, brought up as a peasant in a Portuguese village, but with an inkling that he is really something more; he assumes the name Don Dionís and goes to the palace of the duke of Aveiro to seek his fortune. The second action involves the duke's daughter Magdalena, who falls in love with "Don Dionís," appoints him her writing-master, and then must delicately encourage him to forget his inferior status and make her a declaration. The third plot is related to the others only in so far as it is the story of Magdalena's sister, Serafina. Serafina hates men and loves acting; but when her unwelcome suitor Antonio has her sketched while she is rehearsing in male costume, and she lights on the resulting portrait, she falls in love with it, not recognizing it as her own.

Antonio turns the situation to his advantage by pretending that the portrait is of Don Dionís, a royal prince in exile, who has loved her from afar and wants a nocturnal assignation. She eventually agrees and Antonio promises to bring Don Dionís along, intending of course to play the part himself. Magdalena, meanwhile, in order to forestall her father's marriage plans for her, decides to commit herself to Mireno-Dionís and offers him an assignation for the same night. There follows a classic climax scene in the darkness, with the *gracioso* Tarso bewildered by the arrival of two gallants each calling himself Don Dionís, and each in turn admitted to the palace. Daybreak brings revelations: Mireno learns that he really is the royal prince Dionís brought up in exile; his father Lauro is opportunely restored to the king's favor; Serafina discovers that she has been tricked, but having yielded her honor to Antonio cannot avoid marrying him, and the play ends typically with one happy marriage and one considerably less promising.

There is plenty of unrealistic conventional material here. The news of Lauro's reinstatement comes pat at the moment of denouement, and the humble hero who turns out to be a prince is a figure of folklore. Serafina's failure to recognize herself in the portrait, even though she knows she has recently worn male clothes, pushes the power of disguise to absurd lengths. Coincidence is also stretched very far in Mireno's assumption of the name Dionís which turns out in fact to be his own, and in Antonio's spontaneous invention of a story about the missing Dionís and his father which similarly turns out to be the truth.

The play's greatest weakness probably lies in the character of Mireno. In the early scenes in his village he is all drive and ambition, conscious of some hidden greatness in himself and anxious to make his name; yet in the palace, when Magdalena's favor offers him opportunities, he becomes diffident and shy. The trouble is that instead of being conceived and allowed to develop as a real person, he has two incompatible roles imposed upon him, the first by the romantic plot, the second by the title and its derivation from a well-known proverb, "It was the devil who brought the shy man to court." He offers a telling example of the danger inherent in plays of intrigue, of approaching a character from the outside and fitting him into a prearranged scheme, rather than letting drama arise naturally from human beings and their situations.

But if Mireno is too much of a formula figure, Tirso showed in the two sisters that he really could create character, even in light comedy of this kind. They are beautifully contrasted, Serafina being the more strongly drawn of the two. She is vivacious and enterprising; she would have liked to be a man, and she adores acting partly because it allows her to dress as one. She it is who arranges a Shrovetide entertainment for her more passive sister, and in rehearsing for it shows her ability to play the parts of a lover and a jealous gallant. Magdalena is apparently more demure and submissive, and when love forces her into action she proceeds in a typically feminine and indirect way. Each girl has one big scene: Serafina when she is rehearsing and extolling the theater, Magdalena when she lets Mireno know her feelings by pretending to talk in her sleep; and each typifies the character of the sister concerned. In matters of love Magdalena's oblique declaration contrasts strikingly with Serafina's forthright "I hate you, Count; I do not love you" (I, 347b).

Yet by the end they have largely exchanged roles. When the moment comes to risk all for love Magdalena does not hesitate, and takes the positive step of inviting Mireno to her room. Serafina has more thought for her honor and only allows herself to be persuaded by Juana who, for all her talk about the indecorum of acting, is quite ready to aid and abet a seduction. Gentle, sly Magdalena wins her man in the end; the more open and forceful Serafina, who wants to be a man and can only love a simulacrum of herself, falls a victim to deceitful cunning. The sisters are perfect foils for each other.

Francisco Ayala in a recent edition of *The Shy Man at Court* has drawn attention to the theme of playacting that runs through the work: Magdalena acts a love-scene between Don Dionís and herself, supposedly in her sleep; Antonio acts a conversation between the other Don Dionís and himself as he prepares to seduce Serafina; and Serafina's acting of a male role is integral to the plot.[3] All these histrionics serve to maintain a pleasing interplay between reality and illusion. In particular the contrast between the main action and the passionate drama Serafina is rehearsing, with its attitudinizing and rhetoric, seems to endow the former with a freshness and conviction that go a long way to counteract its many artificialities.

Another contrast is touched on in this play, if only superficially: the well-worn Renaissance topic of opposition between court and countryside. Mireno takes with him to the palace his rustic henchman Tarso, whose uneasiness there is symbolized by the constant difficulties he has with his unfamiliar breeches. Tarso the simpleton *gracioso* is counterbalanced by Vasco, the clever, urban type of fool, who makes the opposite journey from town to village, and whose patronizing flirting with the wench Melisa recalls the wooing of Touchstone and Audrey.

The Shy Man at Court has a surprising number of features in common with *As You Like It*, a play with which it will easily stand comparison. It has no winter wind and no melancholy Jaques, since it is the work of a man coming up to his prime who has not yet known disillusion. But from Serafina's exaltation of drama as the image of life it is perhaps not too long a step to Jaques' complementary realization that all the world's a stage; and the Tirso who here seems to be celebrating the beginning of his long love affair with the theater was certainly in his time to play many parts.

III Don Gil de las calzas verdes (Don Gil of the Green Breeches)

When *Don Gil of the Green Breeches* was put on in Toledo in July 1615 Lope de Vega, writing about it to a friend, called it a "silly comedy by the Mercedarian."[4] In *The Country Houses of Toledo* Tirso himself acknowledges that, whereas *The Shy Man at Court* had been received with general applause all over Spain as well as in Italy and the New World (I, 136), *Don Gil* did not go down well; though he attributes this to the fact that the heroine was played by an actress too old and fat for the part (II, 206). Most modern critics have disagreed with Lope and rated it very high among comedies of intrigue.

The very name "Don Gil" would alert the audience to some kind of pretence, since Gil was a rustic name that went oddly with the title of "don." Sure enough, the name Don Gil de Albornoz has been assumed by Don Martín, a young philanderer who, having seduced Doña Juana in Valladolid, has now come to Madrid to woo the richer Doña Inés and conceals his real name in order to put Juana off the scent. But Juana is always one step ahead of him. She too comes to Madrid, dressed as a man, and makes contact with Inés before Martín can, charming both Inés and her cousin Clara by her dainty appearance and the green breeches she always wears. Martín is bewildered to find that the character he thought he had invented really exists, and is moreover his rival.

Inés is also puzzled by the existence of two Don Gils, but Juana, to make sure she does not settle for the wrong one, now converts herself into a Doña Elvira, who tells Inés what is virtually the true story of Juana's own love affair, except that she changes Martín's name as well as her own, calling him Don Miguel. There is now therefore a Martín-Gil-Miguel as well as a Juana-Gil-Elvira, and it is becoming almost as difficult for the audience as it is for Inés to distinguish illusion from reality.

Yet there are many more complications to come. Clara confesses her love to Juana-Gil and extracts a promise of marriage from "him." Juana-Gil also pretends to be in love with Juana-Elvira and even writes her a love letter, which Inés intercepts. She is almost trapped by her own fabrications when Inés indignantly accuses her of philandering; but Juana's charm and resourcefulness are equal to the occasion.

Meanwhile she has had false reports brought from Valladolid, first that she is pregnant, then that she is dead; so that Martín, driven to distraction by the omnipresent yet elusive Don Gil—since "he" can always avoid a confrontation by turning into Elvira—concludes that poor Juana has become a ghost, and that it is her soul in torment that is haunting him. The transformation of Martín from a cocksure, fortune-seeking young man into a nervous wreck in terror of the supernatural is one of the funniest things in the play.

He may well declare, in the refrain to an almost pathetic soliloquy, that "there is never lacking a Gil to persecute me" (I, 1649b–50a); for by this time Clara and also Inés' former suitor Juan have each decided to further their own cause by pretending to be Don Gil and turning up in green breeches; so that in the climax scene there are no fewer than four characters all claiming to be Don Gil. The audience knows that no Gil really exists; but Martín's invention seems not only to have acquired a malevolent life of its own, but to multiply incessantly, while Martín, like the Sorcerer's Apprentice, can only look on in helpless terror. The farce is brought to an end by the arrival of Juana's father, to whom she can confess the truth, sure now that Martín will be only too relieved to find her alive and marry her.

It must be admitted that Lope had some slight grounds for calling this a silly play. The initial situation is no more farfetched than that of many another comedy of intrigue, but much of the subsequent scheming and disguise is very thinly motivated. Lope himself would probably have taken more care over the contrivance of his plot. *Don Gil* lacks the delicate artistry of *The Shy Man at Court*. The popular figure of the actress in male costume, for instance, is introduced into the earlier work in an unusual way, and in close conformity with the personality of the character concerned; here Juana is just the stereotype of the jilted but determined girl who dresses as a man in order to go out and win back her lover—a commonplace in the Golden Age theater, especially that of Tirso.

Yet even if Juana is only a type, she is attractively presented. The language of the play is always lively, and the situations are hilarious. If one looks at *Don Gil* less with the analytical eye of the literary critic, and more with the ready sympathy of the spectator in the

Intrigue and Illusion

theater willing to be entertained, one can hardly fail to judge it a success. It may be only a farce, but as farce it certainly comes off.[5]

IV La celosa de sí misma (Jealous of Herself)

Internal evidence assigns *Jealous of Herself* to the early 1620s: the Plaza Mayor of Madrid, completed in 1619, is still fairly new, but the Guzmán family with Olivares at its head is already in power. There is also a reference to the new popularity of blue eyes and to the claims of some charlatan to be able to dye black eyes blue; similar allusions are found in a number of plays of 1622–1623.

Again in this play a provincial young man has come to Madrid to contract an arranged marriage with a rich girl; but Don Melchor, from León, is not as unprincipled as Don Martín from Valladolid. On his way to his bride's house he attends mass, and there glimpses a beautiful white hand, whose owner keeps the rest of her person, including her face, decorously hidden behind her cloak. He manages to engage the girl in conversation and arrange a meeting for the next day; and so enthralled is he by her lovely hand that Magdalena, his intended bride, leaves him quite cold, and he confesses honestly that he cannot go ahead with the marriage.

His servant suspects, and the audience knows, that Magdalena and the unknown lady are one and the same; but Melchor will not believe this. Magdalena's hands when openly on view have no attraction for him; it is the cloak, the mystery, and the forbidden thrill that lend them all their erotic power.[6] There is great humor in the way Melchor pours scorn on the very hand he had so recently lauded to the skies; and there is also something pathetically human about his clinging to an illusion that brings confusion and misery, when the truth that could make him happy is already in his grasp. Blanca de los Ríos is right to see a hint of poetry and genuine romanticism in this rejection of the available and the preordained in favor of a chimera (II, 1436).

Magdalena's situation is a piquant one too, at the same time loved and slighted by the man she expects to marry. She is involuntarily cast in two roles, one the rival of the other; and she must continue to play the part of the mysterious stranger if Melchor is not to go straight back to León and out of her life. A sedan-chair bearer, questioned by Melchor's servant and anxious to earn a tip, invents for her the identity of the Countess Chirinola, with an estate and relatives in Italy whither she may be summoned back at any moment. This keeps Melchor on tenterhooks and pressing in his pursuit.

Further complications, of a much more conventional kind, occur when Magdalena's neighbor Angela also falls in love with Melchor, and in her turn assumes the guise of the Countess Chirinola in order to win him. Melchor, who had previously thought there were two women where there was only one, now finds that where he had thought there was one there are two; and as he hesitates between them Magdalena is in danger of losing him in her second role as she has already lost him in her first. The expected night scene ensues, with Magdalena on her balcony reasserting herself by acting two parts to Melchor down in the street below, and explanations follow when the charade has gone on long enough.

This play therefore has its quota of deceptions and disguises; though the discreetly concealing cloak of Magdalena, who is well behaved and only thrust by circumstances into role playing, contrasts significantly with the masculine breeches of the go-getting Doña Juana. Yet illusion of a different kind is more fundamental here. The play rests on Melchor's stubborn belief that the elusive ideal is more desirable than the unconsidered reality within his grasp. There is little doubt that Tirso is satirizing idealism, particularly that of the outdated Neoplatonists. Melchor's obsession is a parody of the religion of love: he first sees Magdalena in church, and her hand becomes the object of his devotion, the image he idolatrously reveres. His very name is that of one of the three kings who came from afar to worship, and one of his first acts is to give a purse full of gold to his lady. But he must learn to open his eyes to the advantages of reality rather than idolize and yearn.[7]

Melchor's romantic idealism is perfectly expressed by the language he uses, which is full of poetic cliché, and more particularly by the contrast between his rhapsodies and the down-to-earth speech of his servant Ventura. Ventura must be one of the sharpest and cleverest of Tirso's *graciosos,* with his torrents of cynical wit. There is amusing bathos during the buildup to the night scene, when Melchor goes to woo his "countess" on her balcony at the hour when the people of Madrid are emptying their slops into the street; Melchor's invocations of heavenly angels are punctuated by Ventura's ironic observations on the pervading "perfumes" and "incense." Magdalena invites Melchor to touch her hand; he cannot

Intrigue and Illusion 53

reach without standing on Ventura's back, and Ventura collapses under the weight. What Melchor falls into is left to the audience's imagination, but the debacle of his upward aspiration is a clever satirical comment on his idealism.

At the height of the complications Ventura exclaims: "Oh, what a fine comedy I would make out of this plot if I were a poet!" (II, 1484b). There seems little doubt that Tirso was well aware what a good play he was writing.

V La fingida Arcadia (Feigned Arcady)

In addition to its passing allusions to Olivares and his family, *Jealous of Herself* also includes occasional hints of satire on contemporary men of letters. Ventura ironically recommends to Melchor the high-flown poetic language of Góngora and his school (1445b–46a); and he later tells Magdalena that her *tramoyas* ("tricks") are like those of an Andalusian poet (1463a). This latter is almost certainly a reference to the southern dramatist Vélez de Guevara, many of whose plays relied on *tramoyas* and *apariencias*, that is, startling effects achieved by the use of stage machinery. These satirical attacks are repeated and given much more prominence in another play of the same period, *Feigned Arcady* (written in 1622).

Ruth Lee Kennedy has analyzed in great depth the background and the literary and political satire of this play, showing how Tirso's hostility to Olivares was linked with dislike of Olivares' protégé Vélez de Guevara and his elaborate stage devices.[8] The play is still a comedy of intrigue, though there are fairly long stretches in which the story gives way to the discussion of literary matters. One senses that its appeal would be less to the general public than to an audience of some literary education—among other things it presupposes a knowledge of Lope's pastoral novel *La Arcadia*—and Professor Kennedy has shown that it was in fact a *particular*, a play written for the entertainment of a noble family and performed privately before them.

The family is that of the Pimentels, who had been influential in the reign of Philip III and were opposed to the new Guzmán ascendancy; the background to the action is the Valtelline campaign of 1620, in which Don Jerónimo Pimentel commanded some Spanish troops; and the occasion being celebrated by the performance is the marriage of another nobleman, Don Felipe Centellas, to an Italian countess. The text records that Felipe had met the countess, Lucrecia, while serving under Pimentel in Italy. How does Tirso convert these simple facts into a play?

He makes Felipe and Lucrecia its hero and heroine, and then for his main substance draws on a work by his master, Lope's pastoral novel *La Arcadia*. Lucrecia is a Lope fan (as she may have been in real life), and is particularly taken by the *Arcadia*; so much so that she has brought all her friends to her country estate in the valley of the Po in order to lead a rustic life as close as possible to that described in the novel.

There are long, impassioned eulogies of Lope and all his writings; but the way in which Lucrecia's friends tease her about her obsession, and the suggestion that she is carrying her admiration a shade too far, reveal a touch of irony on the part of the author. This is no longer quite the unconditional discipleship of *The Country Houses of Toledo*. The slight ambiguity of Tirso's attitude toward his master in this play makes it a text of great interest for the history of the relations between them. After the panegyric of *The Country Houses* there has been some cooling off on Tirso's part, and in the light of a hint about Lope's ingratitude (II, 1391), it seems probable that Tirso was by now expecting more recognition from Lope than the latter was ready to give. In 1621 Lope had dedicated a play to Tirso in his sixteenth *parte*, but in his long poem *Filomena* of the same year had omitted Tirso's name from a roll call of the famous poets of the day. Three years later, in *Antona García*, Tirso will be openly critical of Lope; for the moment he is content with a sly undercurrent to his praise.[9]

At the beginning of the play a typical comedy pretence is already being enacted, for Felipe has left the colors to be with Lucrecia, and while waiting for her to acknowledge him openly as her betrothed has assumed the role of Tirso, her gardener. Her friend Alejandra suspects that "Tirso" is not what he seems, and takes hold of his hand to see if it is really that of a working man. Lucrecia sees the incident and misinterprets it, accusing Felipe of faithlessness. She is about to bestow her own hand on Carlos, another suitor, but Felipe rushes forward to separate them before leaving the palace in dudgeon.

Lucrecia, in despair at his absence, now decides to do what one of Lope's shepherdesses would have done and go mad for love. She starts to behave as though she and those around her really were characters from the *Arcadia*, giving them all the appropriate names. A second layer of pretence is thus laid down; madness, real or feigned, being another common source of illusion in the comedy of intrigue. News of her madness reaches Felipe and brings him hurrying back. He has acquired a servant, Pinzón, and the *gracioso* thus makes his appearance unusually late in the play, in the middle of Act II. Pinzón pretends to be a doctor, and with a flow of Latin jargon and with Felipe in a new role of medical student, sets about curing the patient who is not really ill. In this way a third layer of pretence is superimposed on the other two.

Pinzón's "remedy" is for the whole company to humor Lucrecia and continue to enact the story of the *Arcadia*, under cover of which she and Felipe resume their secret courtship. But it is at this point that Tirso lets the action lapse in order to introduce his polemics. First a game is played in which the men have to improvise verses on given subjects. All are skillful and witty, and none more so than Felipe's sonnet on a toothpick, full of ingenious conceits. Then, developing an idea from *The Country Houses*, Pinzón conjures up a spectacle representing the Parnassus of Apollo. This is divided, like the stage of a medieval mystery play, into hell, purgatory, and heaven. In purgatory are the Gongorists, Latinizers, and pedants; they deserve punishment, but less so than the occupants of hell, those dramatists who in default of talent fill their plays with ridiculous scenic effects. Heaven is reserved for those who write sweetly and naturally, keeping the audience amused with no more stage properties than "a letter, two ribbons, a glass of water, or a glove" (II, 1422b).

The plot has still to be rounded off, and Tirso contrives this with echoes of Act I. Alejandra again has her suspicions, and again through a misunderstanding Lucrecia thinks Felipe loves Alejandra, and prepares to give her own hand to Carlos. Then comes the masterstroke: Felipe arrives to separate them, not on his own two feet as before, but descending from the heavens in a *tramoya*, while another one whisks Carlos up aloft. Thus the level of the main action is fused with the level of Pinzón's magic, and Tirso makes his satirical point in the cleverest possible way. Then, as one illusion after another is peeled away, it is all seen to have been a game. Lucrecia is not mad, and Felipe is neither the shepherd Anfriso, a medical student, or a gardener. The scene is not Arcady, nor even the Po valley, but Madrid, where Don Jerónimo Pimentel has just arrived to witness the marriage of his friends. If *The Shy Man at Court* used the device of the play-within-a-play to lend an illusion of reality to its main action, *Feigned Arcady* ends by breaking the illusion of the theater altogether, and stepping down from the boards to become real life.

The fact that in this play Felipe adopts a pseudonym that is also that of the dramatist himself inevitably gives rise to speculation. There are several Tirsos, and Tarsos, in the works of the Mercedarian, and some of them certainly seem on occasion to be speaking personally for him. *Feigned Arcady* is one of the plays that Blanca de los Ríos relied on heavily for her theory of Tirso's noble birth. Just as she sees a reflection of Tirso in Mireno's consciousness of hidden greatness, so she attaches great importance to Alejandra's challenge to Felipe to admit that his coarse homespun conceals a gentleman (1402a). This is of course part of the plot, and Felipe goes on to deny what is in fact the truth; yet one cannot quite escape the feeling of some intended connection between the character and the dramatist, especially when Felipe, inventing a past for himself, goes on to say that he had studied to be a priest (1403a). There may have been some private joke, known to Tirso's friends in the audience; or could he even have been playing the part of Felipe himself? At all events the link is certainly too tenuous to bear the weight of Doña Blanca's romantic theory.

Tirso was perhaps slightly disingenuous in suggesting that he did not normally use *tramoyas* himself, since a handful of his plays do require them.[10] It may also be objected that there is no more than a difference of degree between the contrivances of the *tramoyistas* and the artificialities of Tirso's own intrigues. Both require suspension of disbelief, and both can give enjoyment to an audience in the mood to accept them. Tirso used the same conventions of disguise and pretence in play after play. The greater part of his extant theater consists of comedies of intrigue, and there are few even of his more serious pieces that do not make some use of the old devices. Yet the four plays studied in this chapter, with their very different uses of illusion, serve to illustrate the variety he was nevertheless able to bring to the repeated application of a formula.

CHAPTER 4

Countryside and Capital

I *The Role of Setting in Drama*

WHEN the Italian dramatists and *novellieri* located their romances in Italy they were giving them a setting familiar to their audience; when English and Spanish dramatists took over the Italianate settings along with the plots the effect was to create an exotic atmosphere that enhanced the mood of fairy tale. No one watching *Twelfth Night* thinks of Illyria as a geographical reality; and the same point is well illustrated by *Feigned Arcady*, where the Po valley represents a midway stage between the total illusion of Arcadia and the reality of the Pimentel palace in Madrid.

But an older dramatic tradition, that of popular farce, had made deliberate use of the familiar and everyday as a source of amusement. One modern successor to this tradition is the English Christmas pantomime, where the comic actor will very often raise a laugh by some reference to a topical event or a local landmark. The reasons why the audience laughs are probably complex. There may be nothing funny about the landmark in itself, but the mention of it sounds amusingly incongruous in a fantastic setting. It also gives the hearers the pleasure of recognition, and a sense of being somehow "in the know"; and it stamps the comedian, usually quite erroneously, as being one of them, and so helps to win their acceptance of him and his clowning.

Lope de Vega was a popular entertainer and knew well how to exploit this appeal of the familiar. In fusing the Italianate type of plot to source material drawn from the history and legend of Spain he not only created a national drama, but enabled himself and his successors to capitalize on their audiences' knowledge and experience, and by providing a semblance of realism in the background make the stories themselves seem less untrue. Thus it is that Golden Age plays are always quite specific in their setting, and when that setting is in Spain frequently confirm it by local references—to the Alcázar of Seville, perhaps, or the aqueduct of Segovia, or, since most plays were written for Madrid audiences, to the streets, squares, and churches of the capital.

The small country towns had their entertainments too, and might sometimes commission a dramatist to write a play, perhaps in honor of a local patron saint; in which case he would certainly put in all the local color he could. However, rustic material bulks too large in the Golden Age theater for this to have been the chief motive of plays about the countryside. The peasant theme has recently furnished Noël Salomon with enough material for a nine-hundred-page book;[1] and it is clear that peasant plays were often written for urban audiences. Often enough, as in the case of Lope's *Fuenteovejuna*, the best of the tales from the old chronicles were about village life. R. O. Jones recently suggested, too, that there may have been an element of deliberate propaganda in the presentation to town dwellers of an idealized rural existence, at a time when it was economically of great importance to stop the drift to the towns.[2]

II La villana de la Sagra (The Village Girl of La Sagra)

Tirso is just as careful as Lope about the locations of his plays, and makes ample use of both town and country settings. An area he must have become familiar with in the years from 1611 to 1615 is the Sagra region of the province of Toledo. This is the setting for his trilogy on Santa Juana de la Cruz, whose home was there; and it is also the scene of a comedy of intrigue, *The Village Girl of La Sagra*, which internal evidence assigns fairly conclusively to the beginning of Tirso's Toledan period.[3]

If Lope had had cause to comment on it he might well have called this a silly play. The intrigue seems unusually preposterous, with the main plot concerning Don Luis, a gentleman from Galicia, who rescues the peasant Angélica from the unwelcome attentions of Don Pedro; Luis falls in love with her himself and gets taken on as her father's beekeeper. In the subplot his sister Inés follows him, in male attire, and becomes page to Don Pedro; later she pretends to be a Doña Juana from Valladolid, and in this guise inspires the love of Angélica's cousin Feliciano. There is an original and amusing twist when in a night balcony scene Inés and Feliciano plight their troth to each other, each thinking that the other is someone else whom they are tricking into marriage; so that twice over the deceiver is deceived. But Act III is unnecessarily and tastelessly prolonged by a mad scene, in which poorly motivated jealousy causes Don Luis temporarily to lose his reason. The mood of this scene is out of harmony with what has gone before, and its language is unusually mannered for this period, so that one might be tempted to see it as a later addition, had not the name Angélica given an obvious cue for an imitation of the *Orlando furioso*.

The chief interest of the piece, however, is its use of rustic motifs and local color. Angélica is first seen in Toledo, where she and others have come in from the country to celebrate the Feast of the Assumption. The next day, 16 August, is the feast of San Roque, and in his honor a *romería*, a kind of pilgrimage-cum-fair, is being held at a little hermitage some two leagues away. Tirso captures perfectly the excitement of the *romería*, with the singing and dancing, the eating and drinking, and the friendly jeering as the contingents from the different villages arrive (II, 128–31); Noël Salomon has an excellent analysis of this scene.[4] More important for Tirso's first audiences, they would know all the places mentioned, and would have behaved in just the same way at *romerías* themselves; and this would doubtless make the rest of the action more credible for them.

Later in the play there is a garden scene (154–57), in which the feigned beekeeper is trying to keep his rival away from Angélica. His talk is all of honey and hives, drones and stinging, but it is full of double meanings, and is easily interpreted by both Angélica and the audience as the language of jealousy and love. Although the song he sings about honey-sweet kisses is a folk song, the country motif is used here in a literary, stylized manner that contrasts nicely with the boisterously popular *romería*.

It must have been round about the time when Tirso was writing *The Village Girl of La Sagra* that Lope produced one of his masterpieces, *Peribáñez*. Although this is a much more serious and moving drama it has some features in common with Tirso's play. In it too a nobleman loves a peasant girl who rejects him, villagers come to see the Assumption processions in Toledo, and the feast of San Roque is duly celebrated next day. Lope, however, goes much further than Tirso in integrating all these elements into the substance of his play. His main character is a farmer, and speaks and feels like one; the religious festivities and the harvest songs are essential to the plot and not added adornments; and right through the play, not in one scene only, the imagery is drawn from the life of the land. A comparison between the two plays shows how Tirso is still at the stage of inserting blocks of rustic material into a preexisting intrigue, rather than letting the drama arise naturally out of a rural way of life.

III La gallega Mari-Hernández (The Galician Mari-Hernández)

The action of *The Village Girl of La Sagra* opens in Santiago de Compostela, and although the characters leave almost immediately for Toledo and La Sagra, the *gracioso*'s fond memories of Galician wines have been seen as a reminiscence on Tirso's part of a visit to Galicia at some time. Firsthand knowledge of the province seems even more apparent in *The Galician Mari-Hernández*. In this play travelers from Portugal comment on just those distinctive features of Galician life that might have struck a visitor from Castile: the hunting of wolves and the herding of pigs, the different method of threshing, the coarse bread made from millet or rye. Dialect words are introduced (for example, *vacoriños* and *carvallo* [II, 80a]), and there is a particularly vivid description of a bear robbing a hive, attacked by dogs and mobbed by the bees but still clinging to his booty (85a); the emphasis placed on this as a spectacle worth seeing suggests that the author may have witnessed it himself.[5]

The story is that of a typical Tirsian pair, a vivacious and determined girl and a weak-willed young man. Don Alvaro originally loves Doña Beatriz, but both of them fall foul of the king of Portugal and Alvaro flees to Galicia. The peasant girl Mari-Hernández comes upon him as he lies asleep; she is in love with him before he even wakes up, and from that moment he has no chance against her. When Beatriz arrives the two women fight over him, while he fluctuates helplessly between them. María wins, as it was obvious she would, by means of the usual misrepresentation and disguise.

The subplot concerning the Portuguese king's oppression of his nobles is basically historical and starts the play off on a serious note, with which the frivolity of the main action jars somewhat. Even María's friend and confidante questions her underhand behavior, and she redeems herself only by the force of her personality and the spirited way in which she takes the sword, to fight first for her own honor and then for Alvaro's life. However, in placing his story firmly in a historical and geographical context Tirso is this time showing some awareness of the importance of that integration of elements of which Lope was such a master. The political struggles in neighboring Portugal explain and justify the Galician local color. The bear also, hanging on to its prey in the face of all comers, seems to be a symbol for the determined Galician girl, and thus to transcend the limits of purely ornamental rusticity.

Tirso's play is not of the same order as Lope's *Fuenteovejuna*, where again a village drama involving nobles and peasants is played out against a background of national events. Nor does Tirso, here or in any other play, approach Lope's great achievement of making the Spanish peasant a heroic figure, investing him with a natural human dignity quite independent of rank. Tirso's villagers are all to a greater or lesser extent figures of fun; even the scintillating peasant girls provoke wonder and amusement rather than any real sense of identification. Tirso always looks on the village slightly patronizingly, from the viewpoint of the court; and his way of showing approval of a peasant character is to elevate him or her to the gentry. This is what happens to Mari-Hernández, whom the king ennobles to make her a suitable wife for Don Alvaro. On the purely technical level of the integration of the setting, however, the play that bears her name marks an advance on *The Village Girl of La Sagra*.

Opinions have varied as to when *The Galician Mari-Hernández* was written. It was performed in the Royal Palace on 24 April 1625,[6] though this could conceivably have been a revival. (It is strange to find a play of Tirso's being put on for the king's entertainment seven weeks after his condemnation by the Committee for Reform; presumably it was already in the repertoire of the company invited to perform, and the full effects of the edict would not be felt immediately.) Blanca de los Ríos thought it was an early play, since the talk in Act I of the expulsion of the Jews by Ferdinand and Isabella seemed to her to refer obliquely to the expulsion of the Moriscos in 1609 as a recent event. Against this, some courtly poetic language and some satirical digs at *tramoyas* that go wrong seem to suggest the 1620s. There are also similarities with *Antona García*, which was probably written in 1623 and retouched in 1625: in each play a Portuguese count woos a Spanish peasant girl in high-flown language while she responds in a brusque, down-to-earth way that is nevertheless full of charm; and in each play the girl is physically strong and brave, and is likened to the *Forneira*, a legendary heroine of Portuguese battles; it would be easy to imagine the same actress playing both parts. It seems likely, therefore, that *Mari-Hernández* is a play of the 1620s, and that its advance on *The Village Girl of La Sagra* is a sign of the author's greater maturity.

IV Marta la piadosa (Pious Martha)

Though Tirso showed some interest in the countryside he was really a townsman, and Madrid was his town. He had been born and had probably grown up there, and despite the better treatment he received in Toledo his thoughts during his early years as a dramatist must often have been of Madrid. He set *Don Gil of the Green Breeches* in the capital, and lent it authenticity with the name and address of the merchant (presumably a well-known figure) to whom Martín was to present his father's letters of credit (I, 1626a), and with the setting of an important scene in the Huerta del Duque. This was the park of Lerma's palace on the Prado, a favorite meeting place for the gentry of Madrid; and *Pious Martha*, another comedy of the same period (1614–1615), also makes use of that venue for one of its scenes.

This is a play in which intrigue goes hand in hand with amusing characterization. Marta is one of two sisters, more closely connected than those of *The Shy Man at Court* since they are both in love with the same man, Don Felipe. The opening scene shows them to be a match for each other in cattiness, but thereafter Marta plots and schemes her way to success, while the duller Lucía is little more than a foil to her. Their father wants Marta to marry an elderly suitor just back from the Indies; but she pretends to have a vocation for chastity and good works, and gets Felipe admitted to the house in the guise of a penniless sick student, on whom she will exercise her "charity" in exchange for Latin lessons.

There are no fewer than five suitors in all for the two girls, which makes for some of the usual complications. But these never get quite out of hand, and the situational humor of an involved intrigue is largely replaced here by the more satisfying humor of character. What makes this play is the ebullient Marta and her mock piety. She is the last person who would ever really feel such a vocation, and this makes her pretence all the funnier, as she throws up her hands in horror at what sounds like indelicate language, lets slip an oath herself then cleverly covers up the mistake, and wheedles her father into letting her go hospital visiting so that she can meet her lover in the Prado; though even the simple father has noticed that "she won't

Countryside and Capital

eat beef as long as there's partridge to be had" (II, 371a). Marta is a wonderful part for a character actress.

Madrid is very much alive in the background to the play, with talk of the Prado, the Huerta del Duque, and the dried-up Manzanares that does not deserve the name of river. But some of the action, including an exciting bullfight, takes place in Illescas, a small town on the road to Toledo. Tirso, living in Toledo at the time, would certainly know this road well, and he introduces a no doubt familiar detail, perhaps even a topical allusion, when he mentions the old houses of Illescas that are falling down (367a).

V   Por el sótano y el torno (Through Basement and Hatch)

The Madrid in which Tirso settled for a few years after his return from the West Indies was a very different city from that in which he had been born. A big building program had been carried through while he was away, and there was now a fine new Plaza Mayor, with a large residential estate to the east of it, stretching beyond the Puerta del Sol to what had been the almost rural Paseo del Prado. The theaters were livelier than ever, and a galaxy of poets had been drawn in to write for them; so that, while voices in the background warned of moral and economic collapse, the cultural life of the capital was lived largely in a heady atmosphere of excitement and rapid change.[7]

This atmosphere makes itself felt in some of the plays of Tirso's Madrid period. Even in the Italianate *Feigned Arcady* he finds room for praise of Madrid, its climate and its culture (II, 1391a); and when the young Don Melchor of *Jealous of Herself* comes to the capital from León, he is amazed by all that he sees, in very much the same way as Tirso himself must have been after his years of absence. The play opens with his words: "What a fine place Madrid is! What an exciting hustle and bustle!"; and he and Ventura comment on the newly modernized houses and the tremendous pace of life in the constantly changing city (II, 1441). In the next scene even a couple of old inhabitants observe how time flies in Madrid, and how difficult it is to know one's neighbors now that everyone lives in apartments (1443). The impression is of a bewildering place from where all stability has gone, and where if mysterious countesses appear and disappear in duplicate that is no more than is to be expected.

It is this same kind of impression that is received by Doña Bernarda, who comes to Madrid from Guadalajara in *Through Basement and Hatch*. In this play Tirso again uses the device of contrasting sisters, but varies it by making Bernarda a widow and the guardian of the younger Jusepa. They are poor, and to find the money for a dowry for herself Bernarda has arranged for Jusepa to marry a wealthy old man from the Indies. He is setting them up in a house in Madrid; but being afraid that his young bride may put his honor at risk, he stipulates that they are to lead an almost enclosed life in it, and that the front door on to the street is to be replaced by a *torno* (a revolving hatch of the kind found at the entrance to a convent) through which goods can be passed without the inmates being seen. They are only to be allowed out in the very early morning to go to church.

Jusepa, however, quickly makes use of this concession to establish contact with the young men from the lodging house across the road; and Bernarda's despairing efforts to keep her in check are frustrated by the fact that she too acquires a suitor, who uses just the same device as Jusepa's gallant of love letters slipped into hawkers' wares. The *gracioso* discovers that the basements of the two houses adjoin, and by knocking out a few bricks a passage can be made through which Jusepa comes and goes, mystifying her sister by her sudden appearances, and passing herself off as a Portuguese lady to explain her presence in the house where she has no business to be. Since both suitors are rich the marriage to the old man turns out to be unnecessary, and Bernarda can capitulate gracefully in the end.

Dr. P. Halkhoree has provided an illuminating analysis of this play, showing how the house itself, with its two points of contact with the outside world, becomes a symbol. The *torno*, at the higher level, represents an unpenetrated enclosure, or a chaste, nonphysical marriage (since it is made plain that the old man is impotent), while the breaking through of the basement wall, from the man's side, suggests a normal sexual relationship. These ideas in turn show up the mistaken sense of values that had motivated Bernarda's original arrangement, and the architecture of the house becomes not merely a basis for intrigue, but a concept essential to the theme of the work.[8]

Dr. Halkhoree's interpretation is borne out by the title, with its emphasis on the house itself; and if the house is important, so is its position. For once we are told exactly whereabouts in Madrid it is: it stands at the Puerta del Sol end of the Calle de Carretas, at the very hub of the city, and its windows look out on to all the main churches and streets; the servant names them one by one as he points them out (III, 557b). There are many references to familiar buildings, from the opening scene outside the inn of Viveros on the Alcalá road to the announcement that precipitates the denouement, the news that the old man has arrived and is putting up at the Oliva inn in the Calle de Atocha. The name Madrid occurs repeatedly, and, more important, the hectic, febrile atmosphere of the capital imbues the whole work. As Bernarda exclaims, "How quickly Madrid has infected my sister with its agitation! Even the wind is contagious here; it destroys everything" (566b). This would surely tickle the audience, who would enjoy being made to feel that they belonged to a swinging city, where dazed provincials could only look on and gape. It is not too much to say that Madrid, like the house at its center, becomes a character in the play, and that in this work of 1623 Tirso has shown for once that he really can integrate action with setting.

VI *The Range of Tirso's Settings*

Tirso traveled widely in Spain, as well as crossing the Atlantic, and was in a position to have painted a number of authentic backgrounds to his plays. Yet Serge Maurel rightly observes that not many of his settings give the impression of a district known at firsthand. Though he nearly always introduces some topographical details, many of these could derive from his source material or from what was common knowledge at the time. Galicia seems to have furnished him with some memories, as does Seville; otherwise it is almost exclusively in the cities and provinces of Toledo and Madrid that he gives the impression of being on known territory.[9]

The reason for this is clear: those were the two cities in which, and for which, the majority of his plays were written. When he was in Alcalá, Segovia, or Guadalajara he was not involved with the theater, nor would these places have the appeal of the familiar for his later audiences. It was therefore his immediate surroundings that he depicted in greatest detail; and the Guadalajara where he made his monastic profession, and attended so many chapters of his order, figures in his theater only as a sleepy provincial town from where young ladies come to be swept off their feet by the infectious excitement of Madrid.

CHAPTER 5

Oddities and Outsiders

I *Tirso's Interest in the Abnormal*

IT has become almost a critical commonplace to say that the Lopean drama is not a drama of profound characterization. It makes relatively little use of soliloquy, and is always more concerned with events than with psychological penetration. In very general terms one may say that Lope de Vega's characters tend to be ordinary people to whom extraordinary things happen; though this is not to deny his masterly power of bringing them to life in their dialogue.

In much of Tirso's theater, as has been seen, the intrigue is uppermost and the characters are little more than marionettes. Yet even within the limitations of this kind of comedy he will sometimes produce a Marta or a Melchor who has some degree of individual endowment; or a Mari-Hernández who, while less individualized, nevertheless shares with other Tirsian heroines an overpowering vitality that raises her above the ordinary.

One character so far encountered goes further than these and shows signs of actual abnormality. This is Serafina of *The Shy Man at Court,* who is not attracted by men, wishes she were a man herself and likes dressing as one, and falls in love with her own portrait. The intrigue is still what matters most, and these characteristics of hers are there to serve the plot; the plot does not arise inevitably out of them. This can be seen from the casual way in which Tirso marries her off at the end to a man she hates, whereas a dramatist really interested in character could have created genuine drama out of her unsuitability for the social life she has to lead. Nevertheless the hints of sexual inversion and of narcissism are there, and they have led critics to see in Tirso an unusual, even a pre-Freudian, interest in deviations from the sexual norm.

A group of characters who have attracted attention in this respect are the various girls who, not unlike Serafina, fall in love with other girls disguised as men: Doña Inés, for instance, who prefers her "little pearl of a Don Gil" to the bearded manliness of Don Martín. Again it is unwise to see too much in this. It is a stock device of Italianate comedy, exemplified also in *As You Like It* and *Twelfth Night;* though Tirso perhaps dwells on the ambiguity more than Shakespeare does. The norm of Golden Age drama, as of most fiction, is heterosexual love leading to marriage, and that is how most of Tirso's plots end. The characters who feel abnormal attractions are always frustrated, and this frustration carries an implied criticism. Yet Tirso's interest in the men and women who do not conform in this respect is sufficient to draw attention to it as a distinctive feature of his theater.

Similarly, outside the religious drama it is assumed that everyone desires wealth, status, and honor. The Golden Age theater may have been attacked for impropriety, but fundamentally it was a theater of the establishment. In contrast with nineteenth-century romantic drama, for instance, it accepts the values of society as a whole and is unsympathetic to nonconformers. Yet here too Tirso occasionally shows a hint of interest in figures cast in a different mold. In his theater an aversion to marriage or a lack of social ambition can be a pointer to genuine individual characterization, and can very occasionally lead to outstanding drama.

II El amor médico (Love Turned Doctor)

One figure who seems at first sight to stand out against accepted values proves to be a conformer after all. This is Doña Jerónima, who in the first scene of *Love Turned Doctor* explains that she has resisted her brother's attempts to get her married off since marriage would interfere with her freedom to study. She prefers Latin to needlework, and her chief love is medicine. She sees marriage as captivity for the woman, and is even more emphatic about the lamentable state of medicine, in the hands of inadequately trained men who are not required to pass even as stiff a proficiency test as those who handle animals (II, 972a).

The first act is set in Seville—it shows some knowledge of the geography of the city, with details about the Alcázar gardens and the Lonja, or Indies Office, just across the road (978b–79a)—and it has often been suggested that the model for Jerónima was a Sevillian poetess, Feliciana Enríquez de Guzmán, who did, according to tradition, pass herself off as a man and study at the University of Salamanca. Tirso may have had Feliciana briefly in mind; but it is hardly necessary to look for any model, since Jerónima does not live up to her promising beginnings.

Even before her outburst on medicine she has given the game away by her curiosity about Don Gaspar, a young man who is staying in the house as her brother's guest but has shown no interest in her. She goes on to watch him through keyholes, read his private papers, and, with face concealed, to make mysterious assignations with him in the Alcázar gardens. In Acts II and III she is in Coimbra, dressed as a man and working as a doctor, so successfully indeed that she acquires a high reputation and becomes physician to the king of Portugal. But it is the pursuit not of medicine but of Don Gaspar that has taken her there. She constitutes no serious answer to the abuses she had deplored, and the medical knowledge she reels off is as garbled and as much for comic effect as that of Pinzón in *Feigned Arcady*. She treats Gaspar's cousin and prospective bride, Estefanía, who of course falls in love with the diminutive "doctor"; then, following the usual pattern, she assumes another female identity, that of the doctor's sister, in which she does finally succeed in attracting Don Gaspar. Even after this the inventions continue, with very little motivation. Her behavior is quite unprincipled and would make one sorry for Gaspar were it not that he switches his affections as many times as she changes her identity—and that, after all, questions of principle are largely irrelevant in this type of play.[1]

Why then does Tirso make Jerónima so potentially interesting at the beginning? Probably chiefly in order to give a new twist to his old device. A girl who can exercise a male profession, however unrealistically, makes a change from so many heroines who simply put on doublet and hose. Tirso more than once expresses his scorn for playwrights who have to borrow plots, and through his namesake in *La ventura con el nombre* (*Fortune in a Name*) he boasts of never being short of them himself (III, 1000b); but what his inventiveness amounts to, as far as the comedies of intrigue are concerned, is a series of endless variations on a very few themes. The situations recur, but there is a constant search for ingenuity of treatment, and Jerónima is a reasonably ingenious figure.

Finding himself with a doctor on his hands Tirso then takes the

Oddities and Outsiders 69

opportunity to express some strong personal feelings about the sorry state of medicine in his day. Jerónima's attack on incompetent doctors is much more serious than the stock antimedical satire which is to be found in Cervantes, Quevedo, and so much of the Golden Age theater including Tirso's own; one wonders if he had recently suffered at their hands. There is another point too at which he momentarily becomes serious and lets a character voice his own feelings: Don Gaspar has been unfairly treated in the past, and he complains vehemently, at quite disproportionate length, about busybodies and writers of anonymous libels (976). This is so clear an expression of personal resentment that it is tempting to connect it with Tirso's denunciation to the Committee for Reform, and to suggest that this passage at least must have been written after that episode.[2] The scenes where the heroine converses in Portuguese certainly seem to place the play in Tirso's later period, alongside *Mari-Hernández* and *Through Basement and Hatch* where the same device occurs.

III El Aquiles (The Achilles)

One of the oddest of Tirso's plays is that in which he dramatizes an episode from the early life of Achilles. The Greek army is gathering to move against Troy, but Thetis wants to keep her son away from the fighting, and so she encourages his love for the princess Deidameia, even to the extent of dressing him as a girl and introducing him into the palace of King Lycomedes as Deidameia's cousin. The princess gradually realizes the truth, and she and Achilles become lovers under the cloak of Achilles' disguise. But Ulysses comes along to shame him into acknowledging his manhood and rallying to the colors. The closing scene takes place outside Troy, where Achilles meets again his old friend Patroclus, is challenged by Hector, and flirts with Polixena while the jealous Deidameia, who has followed him dressed as a soldier, looks on. All ends abruptly *in medias res*, when Ulysses, speaking for the author, concludes the First Part and invites the audience to return next day for the Second. This Second Part has not survived, but it must be supposed that the two together would have given less of an impression of shapelessness than does the First Part alone.

This is Tirso's one play on a classical subject; its chief source is probably the unfinished *Achilleis* of Statius, which deals with precisely this phase of the hero's life and includes the female disguise and the love affair with Deidameia. There is a serious theme in the struggle between love and war to which Achilles is a prey.[3] This is foreshadowed in the opening scenes, when Ulysses himself feels a similar tension between the call to Troy and the claims of Penelope; and it is suggested again on the last page, even after Achilles has opted for war, when Hector and Polixena each throw him down a glove, the one as a challenge and the other as an amorous favor. There is some imposing rhetoric, particularly in a long speech in which Achilles-Nereida defends the claims of "her" other self (I, 1829); Blanca de los Ríos rightly describes the peroration here as Calderonian. Other passages of *culto* writing mark this as a play of Tirso's later period; for example, when Achilles carries the swooning Deidameia to a stream saying "I will revive crystal with crystal" (1811b), he is echoing Góngora's use in the *Polifemo* of the same generic word "crystal" for both clear water and a woman's white flesh.

Much of the *Achilles*, however, is well-worn dramatic convention. There is a typical mad scene when Ulysses tries to escape his dilemma by pretending to have lost his reason. There is playacting when Achilles gets Deidameia, who still thinks he is Nereida, to feign a love scene with him. There is even the familiar joke of a disguised character inspiring love in someone of his own sex. Much of the appeal of the subject for Tirso must have been the opportunity to give yet another new twist to the old pattern of impersonation and intrigue.

Through all this there is no doubt that Achilles really is a man. He is slightly ashamed to adopt his mother's scheme in the first place. He despises the effeminate Lisandro, brandishes a sword, shocks Deidameia by uttering oaths, and provides the play with its humor in his clumsy attempts to walk on high platform soles and handle an embroidery frame.

And yet the play is shot through with sexual ambiguity. To begin with, the stage directions make it plain that the part of Achilles is played by a woman. The reversal of the usual pattern of transvestism is a daring one, and it is probable that an audience of the time would have found the appearance of a real man in women's clothes insulting to the notion of masculine honor.[4] Achilles-Nereida tries to explain away "her" virile behavior by saying that "Nature intended to make me a man, but changed her mind; she made half a man but kept back what was lacking, finishing me off as a woman. . . . I am a

Oddities and Outsiders 71

woman in my face and a man in everything else" (1826a). These are simply invented explanations, but such words, uttered by a woman playing the part of a man who is pretending to be a woman, cannot fail to have strange overtones.

Once Deidameia has understood the hints and become Achilles' mistress the ambiguity becomes stronger than ever. Lisandro, puzzled by the close intimacy between the princess and "Nereida," raises the question of lesbianism (1832b). (This is one of the very few references to homosexuality found in the Golden Age theater.) There soon follows what seems to be a demonstration of it, as Achilles-Nereida lies with his head in Deidameia's lap while she strokes and braids his hair. The apparent eroticism of this scene is extraordinary in a theater in which lovemaking on the stage usually consists at most of the gracious concession of a hand to kiss; and again it might have been hardly tolerable in performance if a real male actor had been involved. One thus reaches the paradox of an enactment by two women of a love scene apparently between two women, shocking in its lesbianism but redeemed by the fact that one is really a man; and equally shocking in its open sexuality but made acceptable by the fact that that man is really a woman after all.

It is not surprising that Tirso never dared to play tricks like these with modern characters. Ancient Greeks were another matter, and he had warrant for the ambiguity both in his source and in the traditional bisexuality of Achilles, who from an early stage in legendary developments of the Homeric figure was the lover of Patroclus as well as of Deidameia, Polixena, Helen, and others. Patroclus makes only a brief appearance in this First Part of Tirso's play, and then merely as an old friend. It is possible that the missing Second Part, which must have dealt with the deaths of Patroclus, Hector, and Achilles, may have been a noble tragedy; what we have mainly in the extant play is comedy of intrigue just beginning to move into serious drama, and built on an unusual case of sexual abnormality.

IV La venganza de Tamar (Tamar's Vengeance)

If the authority of Greek legend allowed Tirso to paint a dubious portrait of Achilles, a higher authority allowed him to go much further in *Tamar's Vengeance*. This is one of five plays that Tirso based on biblical material, and it tells the story narrated in 2 Samuel 13, of Amnon's incestuous rape of his half-sister Tamar and his subsequent death at the hands of Absalom. Just as artists anxious to gain practice in the painting of nudes were able to do so without offense by choosing scriptural subjects like Susannah and the elders, so Tirso can depict a thoroughly and disastrously abnormal character under the protection of a Bible story; and the result is a fine and moving tragedy.

Once again conventional material is included. Amnon (or Amón in the form used by Tirso) is enraptured by a beautiful voice he hears singing in the palace garden, and makes contact with its owner by pretending under cover of darkness to be a gardener. On managing to kiss the lady's hand he quotes the same song about honey and kisses sung by Luis in *The Village Girl of La Sagra*. Later he tries to calm his passion by getting Tamar to play a feigned love scene with him. She, after the rape, laments her lost honor like any Golden Age heroine; and the scene of Absalom's sheepshearing, with its rustic atmosphere and popular songs, could have belonged to the background of any peasant play.

Much more noteworthy, however, is Tirso's close adherence to his source, and his way of developing dramatic substance out of merest hints in the biblical narrative. From the mention of Tamar's "garment of divers colors" he derives the discussion among the ladies about the dresses they are going to wear at a wedding, as a result of which Amnon is later able to identify the crimson-clad Tamar as the owner of the beautiful voice. From Tamar's baking of cakes he draws the conceit of love as an appetite for food, a conceit sustained through repeated use of such words as "dish," "mouthful," "seasoning," "taste," and ultimately "poison"; this is no new idea, and it is found, as Asensio has shown, in a number of Tirso's plays,[5] but it is used here with particular insistence and aptness. And out of Amnon's lovesickness and morbid desire Tirso develops what is probably one of his finest pieces of characterization.

He makes the episode slightly less distasteful by letting Amnon conceive his passion in ignorance. It is aroused by a voice singing in the darkness; only later does Amnon discover that the singer was his half-sister, and by that time he cannot control it. This device also enables Tirso to characterize Amnon before his falling in love, which the biblical narrative does not, and from the beginning he is shown to be odd. He does not share other men's love of fighting, or of women, and is proud of his eccentricity: "I am singular in everything" (III, 363a). He is less sociable than his handsome and extrovert brother Absalom, and has some fault to find with each of the girls mentioned by the other young men. When they go off to make love or to gamble he will read poetry.

He gets his love of verse from his father David, the psalmist, but he has not inherited David's amorous tendencies. The mention of these annoys him, and one begins to suspect that his own lack of interest in women may be an unconscious repression of something he despises in his father. The idea of incest is hinted at when Absalom confesses himself attracted to one of David's concubines, and says his own mother is the only one of the harem he would respect; Amnon is deeply shocked. But all this talk of women has had its effect on him, and instead of settling down with a book of poems he decides to steal into the garden under cover of darkness to spy on the ladies of the palace. He never thinks that Tamar may be among them, and he allows her beautiful singing to melt his resistance to love.

The night is dark, there are storm clouds about, and the garden air is hot and heavy; everything in the atmosphere contributes to tension and overcharged emotion. The background here serves a realism which is not geographical but psychological; and the erotic mood is prolonged by the wedding next day. Background also plays an important part in Act III. Tamar has been raped, and, as in the Bible story, Absalom plans to avenge her by inviting Amnon to a sheepshearing festival on his farm and killing him when he is drunk. The atmosphere of the sheepshearing is all springtime freshness, contrasting with the earlier thundery heat. Streams are flowing, flowers are growing, and the girls who sing are not ladies of the court but unadorned village beauties. Amnon, who has passed through revulsion for Tamar, abjection and repentance, now enters into the happy mood and flirts with the shepherdesses. It seems as though his yielding to his morbid sexuality, and his father's forgiveness, have brought him to terms with the conflict in his nature, and he is no longer singular. Yet ironically it is now that he must die. The atmosphere and the setting serve this time to create suspense through contrast, and the merriment of the scene throws into relief both the bitterness of the changed Tamar and the horror of the final spectacle.

Tirso has a real playwright's gift for recognizing dramatic potential in his sources. He accepts the challenge of the unnatural Amnon, gives him psychological credibility, and makes of him one of the outstanding characterizations of his theater.

Other aspects of this fine play will be examined in the next chapter.

V El melancólico (The Melancholic)

Already in the title of *The Melancholic* there is evidence of an interest in character.[6] The seventeenth century still held to the theory of humors, the belief that a man's personality was determined by the different proportions in his makeup of the four humors of blood, phlegm, choler, and melancholy. The sanguine man was cheerful and outgoing, the phlegmatic man cold and stolid, the choleric excitable, and the melancholic studious and withdrawn. This last is the temperament of Rogerio, who has distinguished himself at the University of Paris and now comes home to Brittany. His scholarliness thus having indicated a certain degree of abnormality, it comes as no surprise to learn that he is not interested in women.

But this is not for long. He sees Leonisa doing her washing in a stream and falls in love with her. Then he learns that he is the illegitimate son of the duke of Brittany and is to go and live at court as the acknowledged heir; but the separation from Leonisa sours this good fortune for him. Leonisa loses her coral necklace, and it falls into the hands of her other suitor, Filipo, who tells Rogerio that she has given it to him as a token of love. Leonisa comes to the palace and has the utmost difficulty in persuading Rogerio that she still loves him. Once he is convinced, they are faced with the problem of the difference in rank between them, and evolve a scheme whereby Leonisa is to be passed off as a Scottish duchess. There follows a conventional impersonation scene, with the *gracioso*, as Leonisa's escort, repeating a meaningless catch phrase in what is meant to be English. This scene is out of harmony with the rest of the play; but it was in any case unnecessary, as word had already come that Leonisa too is of noble birth, and so can marry Rogerio.

The true flavor of *The Melancholic* can best be experienced by comparing it with its source, also by Tirso, *Esto sí que es negociar (That's Business!)* (see note 7 to Chapter 2). This latter is a straightforward comedy of intrigue. In it Rogerio lightly transfers his affections from Leonisa to his noble cousin Clemencia, and goes off to court with never a backward glance. Leonisa takes most of the usual steps to win him back, and her disguise is much more central to the plot. She manipulates the action, and Rogerio becomes a helpless pawn in her hands.

The Rogerio of *The Melancholic* is a very different figure. He resents being translated to the court, since he had always wanted to succeed by his own efforts and win fame for his intelligence and learning (I, 94b). It is true that he almost immediately unsays these words by admitting that his real reluctance is to leave Leonisa; yet he always retains his fundamental seriousness, and his consciousness of being a *sabio*, a wise and learned man. He shows himself capable of dealing sagely and wittily with the various petitioners who come to the palace (thus incidentally providing the opportunity for some social satire on modern fashions and behavior, which helps to date the play in the 1620s); and he reaches his greatest heights in preparing himself to yield Leonisa to the man he thinks she loves: "I crown my suffering by my self-conquest" (114a).

Leonisa too behaves with much more dignity than her counterpart in *That's Business!* Although less individualized than Rogerio, she shares with him the power to make a noble renunciation when she thinks she is beneath him in status: "My love is not desire, but a power of the soul; and to love for love's sake alone is perfection, if it is also martyrdom" (104a). This hint of Neoplatonism matches the philosophy of Rogerio, who has proclaimed himself a "man conversant with Plato" (88b). Within a framework of conventions—the love at first sight, the two revelations of identity, the fatuous impersonation—this is a more adult play than most, in which the main characters are credited with serious emotions, and in which individual characterization of an unusual kind for once overshadows intrigue.

VI *Possible Personal Echoes*

To say that a character is individualized is by no means to suggest that he or she is necessarily true to life. Tirso's early critics made much of the humanity and verisimilitude of his creations, particularly the engaging heroines, and speculated about the source of his knowledge of feminine psychology. One suggestion often put forward was that he might have acquired it through hearing confessions; though the number of women who can have confessed to the kind of thing his heroines get up to must have been small indeed. Nowadays it is clear that though he could put strongly marked personalities on the stage there is very little question of his characterization being closely lifelike. The world of his theater is a literary world, and most of his figures have their origin in generalized literary convention or in earlier writings. This is certainly true of those who display abnormal sexuality, of whom the most fully developed—Amnon—is also the one with the most explicit source; and it would be a mistake to try to explain these figures by postulating anything about Tirso's experience of life, still less about his own psychological makeup.

The one abnormality that can perhaps be seen as having some autobiographical relevance is the melancholic Rogerio's professed desire to be a self-made man, disingenuous though this turns out to be. Rogerio's long speech (94b) is a noble utterance. His ideal had always been the golden mean. He loved reading and the solitude of the countryside, and was thankful that though he lacked inherited rank and wealth he was able to aspire through his own industry to a fame and greatness born of talent and a studious life. His new rank has paradoxically belittled him, since it has equated him with fools. Few men of power have been noted for their intelligence. He will now lose his reputation for wisdom, and thinks status a poor exchange for the talent which aspires to soar. The key word of this speech is *ingenio*—talent, cleverness—which occurs six times, twice in connection with *volar*, to fly.

There are obvious coincidences here with the shepherd Tirso in his little boat at the country house regatta (see p. 19 above). The device on that boat involved a flight up to the laurel wreath of fame on the two wings of talent and study; and there was no doubt that Tirso was there writing about himself. There would seem, therefore, to be something of him also in the studious Rogerio, who contrasts his own intelligence with the wealth and power of stupid men, and never forgets that he is a *sabio*.

It is not surprising that Blanca de los Ríos saw in Rogerio's illegitimacy another reflection of what she believed to be Tirso's own personal drama. It is not necessary, however, to carry the author's identification with his character as far as this. Unrecognized children and revelations of identity are stock ingredients of folktale and romance, and thence of the comedy of intrigue, and in this respect Rogerio is pure literature. He disappoints our expectations by admitting that he really does enjoy prosperity and is only sad because he misses Leonisa. But in one memorable scene he has spoken for Tirso, and this unusual choice of an intellectual as hero of a comedy is one of the more noteworthy pieces of Tirsian characterization.

CHAPTER 6

Forgiveness and Friendship

WITH the exception of *Tamar's Vengeance*, in the plays examined so far few serious moral considerations arise. It is possible to criticize some of Tirso's heroines for their impropriety, as certain of his contemporaries did; a modern reader might take greater exception to their outrageous untruthfulness. But this is to apply moral standards that are no more appropriate to escapist entertainment of this kind than they would be to a Feydeau farce; the comedy of intrigue is amoral, not immoral. The plays themselves sometimes contain implicit criticism, for instance of arranged marriages or unfaithful lovers, or explicit criticism in the form of social satire; but little of this goes beyond the conventional. A number of Tirso's plays do however treat moral questions, and the titles of some suggest a moral lesson as their very starting point.

I   El celoso prudente (Jealous but Prudent)

The principles guiding the behavior of most characters in Golden Age drama are those embodied in the rigid code of gentlemanly honor, which required a man at all costs to protect his public reputation and that of his family, and a woman to have no dealings with a man except in marriage or under the binding promise of it. Compared with his contemporaries Tirso makes relatively little use of this code in his plots, and his treatment of questions of honor distinguishes the morality of his theater somewhat from theirs.

One of the petitioners who seeks Rogerio's help in *The Melancholic* is a man with an unfaithful wife. Rogerio's advice to him must have surprised the audience: suffer in silence, and spend all the money you can on her to stop her going to others for it (I, 111a). Don Sancho of *Jealous but Prudent* is by no means as conciliatory as this, but the lesson he learns, and passes on at the end of the play, is one of extreme caution where honor and vengeance are concerned: "Let the man who is jealous as I was keep his counsel and wisely verify his suspicions, which will often prove false as mine did; and if they are justified let him exact vengeance in secret, for once his dishonor is known it will be on everybody's tongue" (I, 1155b).

Don Sancho de Urrea is the Spanish husband of Diana, elder daughter of a Bohemian nobleman. Her sister Lisena is secretly betrothed to Prince Sigismundo. Their father has been aware of the prince's attentions but thought they were directed toward Diana; he therefore marries her to Sancho in order to ward off the prince, and failing that, at least to keep his own family honor intact, since Diana will now be Sancho's concern. Sigismundo is threatened with a dynastic marriage to a Hungarian princess, but continues to see Lisena. In order to protect her sister Diana had allowed her father to persist in his mistaken belief, and even now lets it be thought that the prince is still wooing her. The little game is meant to be kept from Sancho, but he becomes suspicious and suffers great distress thinking himself dishonored. He decides to kill Diana and the prince, and is only waiting for an opportunity to do so secretly so as not to publicize his shame; he plans to stage two apparently accidental deaths, by drowning and by fire. But the truth comes to light just in time. Lisena and her prince connive with the Hungarian princess, who in any case prefers Sigismundo's younger brother; Lisena impersonates her and marries Sigismundo, and Sancho thankfully recognizes his wife's innocence.

The play is a hybrid like *The Melancholic*. Sancho's mistake arises entirely out of implausible impersonations and misunderstandings of the conventional kind, yet the treatment of his jealousy is serious and almost tragic. The need for secrecy means that he cannot confide in anyone else, and for once soliloquy is in place. Tirso gives him no fewer than four splendid monologues, in which he reflects on his personal honor as a Spaniard, a soldier, and a man of upright life, deplores the harsh laws that make his reputation hang on the fragility of a woman, and tries to reason in his tormented mind about what he should do. Through Act III he rises to a crescendo of rhetoric, and develops the conceit of honor which is sick and can only be cured by the letting of blood. (Calderón borrowed this grim conceit, along with Sancho's situation as husband of a woman previously loved by a prince, for his own great honor tragedy *El médico de su honra*.)[1]

Jealous but Prudent is the play about which Tirso writes so triumphantly in *The Country Houses of Toledo,* challenging the moralists to find fault with it if they can (see above, p. 33). One might perhaps point out on their behalf that Diana acts foolishly and dangerously in allowing anyone to think that she is unfaithful, and that Sancho is quite prepared to kill and delays only for selfish motives, not from any higher principle. Yet it remains true that all the characters are generous and well intentioned; that the two sisters, as well as the two brothers, act only for each other's good and without any hint of jealousy or rivalry between them; that the love of Lisena and the prince is tender and constant; and that Sancho, in seeing how "the harsh laws of this world are an impediment to the laws of God" (1141b), has glimpsed an important truth about the inadequacy of the code of honor. Tirso was largely justified in his claim to have produced a superior type of play.

II Honor and Forgiveness in Tamar's Vengeance

The title of *Tamar's Vengeance* identifies it as a play about the code of honor. Amnon's rape of his half-sister has robbed her of her honor; it cannot in this case be restored by marriage, only by the death of Amnon, and Tamar appeals to her father David to execute justice. But David is also the father of Amnon, and experiences an agonized conflict: "Justice appeals to me as king, love as father" (III, 393a). When Amnon comes to kneel trembling before him he can only turn away, remembering God's forgiveness of his own sin with Bathsheba.

Tamar's cause is taken up by Absalom who is her full brother, and who is moreover jealous of Amnon's position as heir to the throne. David recognizes Absalom's ambition and the selfishness of his motives, and his sympathies are now wholly with his eldest son, whom he sees as Abel to Absalom's Cain. After the murder of Amnon Tamar can hold her head high again, "for the blood of the traitor is the blazon of the innocent" (403b), but the last word is with David who can only weep at the outcome of this "piteous tragedy" (404b).

The Bible story furnishes Tirso with the emotions of his characters as with the actual events, yet he draws unexpected drama and meaning out of it. The central character of Act III is none of the three children but David, who is old and wise enough to see beyond immediate questions of clear-cut right and wrong. Amnon's deed was not a self-contained act, but one link in a chain of sin and error. It led to his killing by Absalom, which in one sense was an act of justice, in another a jealous and treacherous fratricide. It has already been suggested that David bore some responsibility for Amnon's warped instincts; whether or not he was conscious of his own sin being visited on his children, he remembered that God had forgiven him and knew he must forgive Amnon—as in due course he will also forgive and weep for Absalom, whose strange death is foreshadowed by many references to his long and beautiful hair.

Dr. A. K. G. Paterson in the perceptive introduction to his edition of this play[2] shows how the sheepshearing setting causes David to think of the dead Amnon as a sacrificial lamb, and he suggests that by the end Amnon has become a prefiguration of Christ. If this is so the ending may be thought to point forward to the Christian dispensation, and to the Cross as the symbol of forgiveness and the only remedy for sin. But as yet the tragedy must remain open-ended, with no clear statement of right and wrong. According to the code of honor Tamar must be avenged; she represents the laws of this world. David represents forgiveness, which is the law of God; and as Don Sancho saw, the two are not compatible.

III Cómo han de ser los amigos (True Friendship)

It is perhaps a little surprising that Tirso let *Jealous but Prudent* bear the burden of his self-justification in *The Country Houses of Toledo* rather than the second of the three plays included in that miscellany, *True Friendship*. This is an early work, known to have been sold to an acting company in 1612, but it was probably retouched when being prepared for the press in 1621. Its title bears witness to its moral standpoint, and its tone almost throughout is elevated and idealistic.

After a change of ruler in Castile Don Manrique has taken refuge across the Pyrenees with his friend Gaston de Foix. Gaston is in love with Armesinda but she does not return his love, and in any case her father the duke of Narbonne has promised her to Don Ramón. Manrique obliges Gaston by killing Ramón in a joust, but this angers the duke, who takes Gaston prisoner while Manrique is forced to flee. Manrique and Armesinda have fallen in love at first sight, and the rest of the story concerns Manrique's answer to the conflicting claims of love and friendship. Though he is encouraged to seize Gaston's estates and win Armesinda for himself he refuses to take advantage of his friend. When Armesinda's sister Violante, who loves Gaston and engineers his release, misleads Manrique into thinking that Gaston loves her, Manrique at last feels free to claim Armesinda; but Gaston has only to appear and disabuse him for Manrique to renounce his own happiness again, even though the pain of doing so temporarily drives him mad. (The mad scene that follows, perhaps the earliest of the many in Tirso's theater, is pathetic rather than tasteless and does not lower the grave tone of the work.) This measure of what Manrique's loyalty has cost him so moves Gaston that he in turn yields Armesinda to his friend, and marries Violante.

This play is much further removed than *Jealous but Prudent* from the standard comedy of intrigue. Lovers' entanglements there have to be, since these form the testing ground for Manrique's friendship; but they are lent dignity by being set against a historical background of tensions between Castile, Aragon, and Navarre, as well as by the behavior of the characters concerned. No one indulges in deliberate impersonation; Gaston makes his escape dressed as a pilgrim, and as such is not at first recognized by Manrique, but the resulting scene is bitter, not humorous. The secondary figure Violante is the only character to do any intriguing. Armesinda remains passive and at the mercy of events, but she becomes heroic in her adherence to Manrique through imprisonment and despair.

Language for the most part is measured and grave, to match the seriousness of the theme. Two typical features of Tirso's drama of moral examples are the soliloquies and the relatively large proportion of scenes in long-lined meters such as the Italianate tercet and *octava rima;* there are five such passages in this play. A certain sententiousness is to be expected in drama which is so openly didactic, but there is also an unusual richness of metaphor, and one image receives particular emphasis: the diamond strength of true friendship, contrasted with the glass of an attachment that breaks under strain (I, 158).

IV   El amor y el amistad (Love and Friendship)

There is little to distinguish the early *True Friendship* from a group of three or four similarly exemplary plays which seem to date from the beginning of Tirso's later period, and of which *Love and Friendship* is one. Ruth Lee Kennedy points to certain coincidences with *The Country Houses of Toledo* (1621), and sees the group as arising out of the turbulent politics of that year, when the old regime was replaced by that of Olivares and questions of loyalty were of immediate concern.[3] Jaime José González and Gerald Wade suggest that *Love and Friendship* might be nearer in date to *True Friendship*.[4] It certainly seems to have grown out of the earlier play; it develops the theme of the testing of loyalty, as well as the diamond-glass conceit. However, *True Friendship* must have been fresh in Tirso's mind in 1621 when he inserted it in *The Country Houses*, and he could well have gone on to write *Love and Friendship* soon afterward.

The diamond-glass opposition has now become a leitmotiv running right through the play; and whereas before there were only diamonds, now the loyal friend and faithful *dama* are contrasted with others who crack when put to the test. The trial this time is deliberate. The count of Barcelona has rewarded Don Guillén's past services by making him his close friend and *privado*. Guillén, having overheard an ambiguous conversation and witnessed some misleading hand kissing, believes that his other friend Don Grao and his lady Estela are in love, and not all their protestations will convince him otherwise. He gets the count to pretend to withdraw his favor, strip him of his estates, and cast him into prison. All the other fawning courtiers and amorous ladies turn away, and only Grao and Estela, ignoring the apparent risk to themselves, come to plead for him.

The hand kissing that had worried Guillén—and it is after all usually a significant and even a committing act in the Golden Age theater—recurs near the end when the count submits Estela to a final test by pretending to woo her himself. This is more than Guillén can bear, and he bursts out of his hiding place to separate them. The coincidence of this byplay concerning hands with the similar episodes in *Feigned Arcady* may perhaps help to confirm a date in the early 1620s.

Monologues again predominate over racy dialogue. So little humor is there that the *gracioso* does not make his appearance until Act III, and even then he figures more as a further example of loyalty than as a source of light relief; though the two ridiculous ladies who vie for the favors of Don Guillén do contribute a little comedy to Act II.

The most memorable character is Estela. She is unshakably faithful and as steadfast in suffering as Armesinda, though apparently colder; this is perhaps because she has no sister or other confidante to whom to express her feelings, and we see only those she chooses to reveal in public. But this solitariness is in keeping with her nature. Don Grao likens her to the rocky Catalan mountains where she loves to hunt (III, 507b); she likens herself to a castle, an oak, a ship riding the storm (546b). In her dignified aloofness from a Guillén who doubts her word she is a Cordelia to the Goneril and Regan of the effusive court ladies. No greater contrast to the stereotyped Tirsian heroine could be found, and the gallery of Tirso's women characters would be very incomplete without Estela.

V Limitations of Tirso's Moral View

The other plays on the theme of loyalty that Professor Kennedy groups with *Love and Friendship* are *Privar contra su gusto* (*The Reluctant Favorite*), *Palabras y plumas* (*Words and Feathers*), and *Cautela contra cautela* (*Cunning Matched with Cunning*); this last is of doubtful authorship, having been published in the Second *parte*, but she finds its similarities with other Tirsian works stronger than those it also bears with the theater of Mira de Amescua. Mira is another dramatist in whom the moral strain is pronounced, perhaps his finest examples in the genre being the pair of plays on Alvaro de Luna that also appeared in Tirso's Second *parte*. This important facet of Tirso's work, so much overshadowed by the more numerous comedies of intrigue, links him with Mira and with Ruiz de Alarcón, and points ahead to the more probing and disturbing moral drama of Calderón.

The world of Tirso's didactic plays is not a consistently moral one. Each play singles out one virtue to exalt, and ignores other deficiencies. Diana's goodwill toward her sister makes her a less than perfect wife. In the cause of friendship Manrique is prepared to ride roughshod over the feelings of the woman he loves, who is allowed no say in the matter of whom she is to marry. (He is also remarkably casual about killing Don Ramón in the lists, as is Violante about having some other prisoner garrotted so that Gaston can escape.) Guillén is so mistrustful and unpleasant to Grao and Estela, and so unfair to the count whom he forces under protest into an objectionable pretence, that one wonders why they all love him so much. But it is as inappropriate to raise such doubts as it is to question the morals of the comedy of intrigue. These weaknesses are all necessary to the plots; they have to be there in order to demonstrate the strengths, and so can be overlooked in a drama in which everything else is subservient to the main theme.

The fact is that in this drama of ideals as elsewhere Tirso's usual practice was to start from a concept. The title, whether it was *True Friendship* or *The Shy Man at Court*, came first, and then the characters were devised and the action manipulated to illustrate the point. It is as though Tirso sets himself a problem in his title, and inscribes a triumphant "Q. E. D." at the end of the play. Calderón in his moral drama is equally concerned to teach a lesson, but he more often lets it arise out of a human situation, however remote in time—Herod's overweening passion for his wife Mariamne, or Semiramis' enslavement of two men—which is why it is more consistently moving than Tirso's. Tirso could on occasion do this too, as *Tamar's Vengeance* shows. Starting there from an existing story of human relationships, he not only brings its protagonists to life but goes on to draw from it truths that speak to his own age, and to others, in an altogether different voice from the predicatory tones of the idealistic drama of moral example.

CHAPTER 7

Monarchs and Ministers

I *Tirso and* privanza

TIRSO has left a brief record of his attempt to follow his own precepts in the matter of forgiveness and conciliation. One of the characters who momentarily speaks on his behalf is Garbón, the *gracioso* of the *Achilles*, who turns up for battle without any weapons but claims to be carrying adequate armor for the battle of life: absence to combat love, patience to confront death, resourcefulness to cope with poverty, and so on. At the end of his speech he becomes more personal: "Against wrongs I carry the forgetting of them. Only against an arrogant fool have I been unable to find any weapon; although they say that the best remedy is to flee his scorn, and so I turn my back on strife and on the fool" (I, 1839–40).

This must be a reference to Tirso's adversary of the 1620s, and in view of the talk of fleeing it was probably inserted at the time of his departure from Madrid. However, even if flight removed him from the scene of battle, the forgetting of wrongs proved to be beyond him. The many mentions of envy and ill-treatment, even as late as in the prologue to the Third *parte*, show that his resentment remained acute. It has been seen that the enemy was almost certainly a protégé of Olivares, and that the hostility was connected with Tirso's opposition to the latter's rule. In this too he was persistent and showed no disposition to come to terms, even though Olivares twice got the better of him. Yet his continued dislike of the *privado* and his friends was more than a personal matter. *Privanza* is an important theme in Tirso's theater, and a study of it reveals a strong idealism behind his political attitude.

The *privado*, or man privy to the king, is the close friend and favorite of the monarch and also the chief minister and ruling power in the country. In days when kings were supposed to be absolute monarchs but often lacked talent for the task to which they had been born, it was only natural that they should attract to themselves men of greater ability who would effectively take the government into their own hands. The *privado* is a man who has risen to the top by a process of natural selection, even if this has also sometimes involved ruthlessness in the elimination of rivals. Tirso does not, at least for a time, condemn the institution of *privanza*, but suggests that power should be responsibly exercised.

References to *privados* are found in his theater from an early stage. One of them had been behind the troubles of Mireno's father in *The Shy Man at Court*. "Lauro," as he called himself in exile, was uncle and guardian to Alfonso V of Portugal, but an enemy insinuated himself into the young king's favor and brought about the uncle's downfall (I, 339b). *True Friendship* begins with an explanation of Manrique's presence in Foix: his father had been *privado* to Queen Urraca of Castile, and so close to her that she even thought of marrying him; but this aroused the opposition of other nobles who replaced Urraca on the throne with her seven-year-old son, and Manrique has now had to flee from a new *privado* (I, 132–33).

Two warnings are implicit in these early examples: it is very easy for an unscrupulous man to gain power, particularly when the king is young and inexperienced; and the position of the *privado*, who is there by neither divine right nor democratic election and will inevitably attract jealous opposition, is an extremely precarious one. These considerations were not especially topical in 1611–1612, even though a *privado* was then in power: government was in the hands of Philip III's minister the duke of Lerma, who in turn had his own favorite, the upstart adventurer Rodrigo Calderón; but they had become topical by the time the two plays were published in *The Country Houses of Toledo*. A teenage king, Philip IV, was now on the throne, and Spain had witnessed some spectacular reversals in the fortunes of mighty men. Lerma fell from power in 1618, unseated by his own son, the duke of Uceda. Uceda's ascendancy lasted only until the death of Philip III in March 1621, at which point Olivares, already a favorite of the new king, was able to seize control. The final demise of the old regime was signaled by the execution of Rodrigo Calderón later that year.

No wonder the theme of fortune's wheel began to figure frequently in the literature of the time. Tirso mentions it more than once in connection with a *privado*. As one who had been on friendly terms with Lerma's entourage the change of regime, just when he had settled in Madrid and was looking forward to a period of personal triumph, affected him greatly. It was also perhaps not without significance for him, in view of the conciliatory note in his theater, that Olivares brought with him an awakening of militarism. In *The Village Girl from Vallecas* (II, 797) Tirso had written lovingly, almost reverently, of Philip III and his "extraordinary gentleness"; and in his *History of the Mercedarian Order* he was to describe him as "gentle, peaceable, saintly and pious" (II, 445); now Olivares was turning against "the supine policies of the Lerma regime" and "the humiliating pacifism of Philip III's Government."[1]

Those of Tirso's idealistic plays that seem to date from 1621 or 1622 all link the display of virtue in some way with the figure of a *privado*. The jealous but prudent Don Sancho de Urrea is *privado* to the King of Bohemia, having won that position through his prowess in battle. Don Guillén of *Love and Friendship* is admitted to the *privanza* of the Count of Barcelona in return for support for his claim to the title, and makes use of the well-known precariousness of royal favor in the test he devises for Grao and Estela. Service, prudence, and loyalty are clearly connected in Tirso's mind at this time with the exercise of power.

II Privar contra su gusto (The Reluctant Favorite)

Privanza receives its fullest treatment in Tirso's theater in *The Reluctant Favorite*, another of the idealistic plays of the same period. Professor Kennedy assigns it to 1621; Professor Wade thinks that the love intrigue involving a lady's garter may be a friendly reference to the Order of the Garter that the Prince of Wales, the future Charles I of England, was wearing during his visit to the Spanish court in 1623, and that the play may have been written for the prince's entertainment in that year.[2] Both critics are agreed that the play reflects an early stage in the Olivares regime, when Tirso was not altogether unsympathetic to the favorite.

Don Juan de Cardona, like Don Manrique of *True Friendship*, is the son of a man who had fallen from *privanza*, in this case from the favor of the king of Naples. By a lucky chance he saves the life of the new king, Fadrique, who sees in him a guardian angel and insists on making him his own *privado*. Don Juan begs to be excused this honor, since he had only ever wanted good fortune in moderation; he exalts *medianía* in much the same terms as the studious Rogerio (III, 1081a), and it is interesting to note that he too is a book lover

(1087a). But this release is the one request that the king will not grant him.

Meanwhile two love intrigues have developed. The king is in love with Juan's sister Leonora and has designs on her honor; while Juan is enamoured of a lady he has glimpsed bathing in the river, and has stolen her garter as a keepsake. The lady was the king's sister, the Infanta Isabela, who on seeing Juan with the garter enjoins him to silence about the episode for the sake of her good name. But through a typical series of inventions and misunderstandings she is led to believe that he has told his friend Luis. Luis and his lady Clavela also come to find their own reputations implicated in the affair, and blame Don Juan. When the king objects to Juan's protection of his sister's honor, and locks him up so that he himself can go a-wooing, it seems that everyone is against Juan, and that a turn of fortune's wheel has dashed him to the ground.

Juan, however, escapes from the locked room and follows the king to try to ward him off Leonora, secreting a bullet in his mouth so as to disguise his voice. Again luck plays into his hands and he is able to unmask a conspiracy threatening the king's life. Fadrique, not recognizing his rescuer in the dark, takes him for a divine emissary—the more so when the "saint" turns out to know all that the king had been up to. Pressed to ask for a reward, Juan makes three requests: Fadrique must not pursue Leonora; he must favor his *privado* less; and some of Juan's honors must be transferred to Luis. Word of the mysteriously well-informed stranger soon spreads through the rest of the company. The fact that he is apparently hostile to Don Juan, as they are, predisposes them in his favor; and when on a later appearance he proves to know all their secrets too, they all come to believe that he is a saint. Having won universal confidence he is able to dispel resentments in the affair of the garter, and to persuade the king to marry Leonora; while he, his real identity established, is rewarded with the hand of the Infanta.

The garter intrigue is as silly as any in Tirso's theater, but it serves two purposes. Its minor function is to provide for the sensuous description of a bathing beauty, in what must be one of Tirso's longest passages of *culto* writing: Don Juan recounts his adventure in no fewer than eleven *octavas*, full of Gongoristic language and classical allusions (1077–78). More important, it leads to the clever situation, akin to that of Magdalena in *Jealous of Herself,* in which the same people revile Don Juan in one of his identities and revere him in the other; and it plays its part in an impersonation which is of unusual seriousness and significance.

Don Juan's three requests to Fadrique on his first "saintly" appearance amount to three pieces of advice: the king should restrain his amorous inclinations; he should limit his favors to his *privado*, who will be all the more likely to retain his position if there is not too great an imbalance between him and his fellow courtiers; and for the same reason other deserving noblemen should also be rewarded. The tone of this important speech leaves no doubt that in speaking of his other self the *privado*, Don Juan is really speaking about Olivares: "He is hateful to everyone now that you have raised him so high. . . . Don Juan for all your praise of him has not the ability to govern the country single-handed. If you relieve him of the burden that now oppresses him, and give him less, you will be more likely to preserve him" (1103a). That the advice to lead a more chaste life is also aimed directly at Philip (whom Olivares was said to be encouraging in his womanizing), becomes apparent when Fadrique speaks of "young kings, tired of authorized deities, calling a truce to majesty and behaving like lovers" (1105-6); Fadrique himself has as yet no "authorized" object for his love, but Philip, young as he was, was already married.

If there is explicit advice for the king, there is implicit advice for the *privado*. Don Juan, divesting himself of some of his honors and giving his personal possessions to pay the king's debts, points the way. He goes even further; in his second "saintly" appearance, when he proves to know the secrets of others and urges them to admit the truth and do the right thing, he becomes a symbol of conscience. This is surely the minister's highest role: to act as conscience to the nation, and set its moral tone. If he can do this he will indeed be a saint, and a worthy successor to the gentle and saintly departed king.

The Reluctant Favorite is a blueprint for monarch and minister at the beginning of a new era, and a play in which intrigue and impersonation are brought into the service of the highest ideals.

III La prudencia en la mujer (Prudence in Woman)

It is only at a late stage in *Prudence in Woman* that the question of *privanza* arises, but the treatment of it then suggests that Tirso's attitude has become more critical. This is a historical play, dealing with the early years of the reign of Fernando IV (1295-1312) and the regency of his mother, María de Molina. She has been left a young widow with an infant son, and has to struggle for his rights against the repeated attempts of ambitious princes to usurp the throne. As long as he is young she gets the better of them, and each time tries to shame them into submission by a more magnanimous treatment than they might have expected. In Act III the king, now adolescent, is beginning to rule for himself, and his mother retires to her country estate. She warns him against *privados*, but Fernando listens all too readily to his scheming uncle, the prince Don Juan, and is ready to believe his mother a traitress, until a final confrontation establishes the truth.

Tirso took most of his material from the chronicles of the period, yet it also had a remarkable topicality in his own day. A masterly study by Professor Kennedy of the play and its background has shown how in detail after detail it reflects events and preoccupations of the early 1620s. A young king—like Philip, the fourth of his name—is on the throne. There is no money to pay the troops, but the queen hesitates to impose even heavier taxes on the productive classes; she sets an example by sacrificing her own possessions, while the nobles continue to enrich themselves. The king, once in power, dismisses the parliament over which he should be presiding in order to go hunting. As minister of justice he takes his cue from his uncle, the new *privado;* he persecutes the loyal Caravajal brothers and has them thrown into prison. Professor Kennedy documents analogies to all these episodes in the early years of Philip's reign.

She shows too how, alongside the new militarism of Olivares, the question of a more rigorous internal policy had become a matter of public debate: was the state better served by suppression of its enemies or by the exercise of mercy? Tirso, as might be expected, favored the latter, and the clemency repeatedly shown by María de Molina is a reflection of this current preoccupation.[3]

There can be no doubt that in this play Tirso is voicing his deep concern about the government of the country. Most of his explicit advice is concentrated in María's Polonius-like admonitions to her son at the beginning of Act III: the king should serve God; not allow *privados* to govern him or to become too rich; treat all his grandees alike; be friendly but not overfamiliar; let himself be seen and loved by his people; not take advice from court entertainers (as Philip was apt to do); respect his armed forces; and finally, a typically Tirsian touch, choose his doctors with care (III, 936b). Professor Kennedy is right to point to this speech as a mirror for princes, and one directed specifically to Philip IV.

Prudence in Woman stands apart from most other Tirsian plays in that its main substance is historical, it has a minimum of comic relief, and no conventional intrigue (though there is plenty of political intriguing). There is virtually no love interest: each of the dissident princes wants to marry the queen for his own ends, and another nobleman, Don Diego de Haro, because he loves her, but she glories in her chaste widowhood and listens to none of them. The play is, however, stylistically akin to the other moral dramas in its long speeches and its dignified tone, to which a number of biblical and classical allusions contribute. An unusual concern for artistry is shown in the opening scene: the queen's speech in *romance,* the short-lined meter of the Spanish ballads, contrasts with the Italianate hendecasyllables used by the nobles, and establishes her as a more genuine and more truly Spanish figure; while the *octavas* with which each prince in turn takes his leave symmetrically balance those with which they had introduced themselves at the beginning.

The absence of a complex intrigue and the recurrent assaults of Don Juan, each in turn foiled by the queen, make for a repetitive story line. The action is episodic, and very nearly unilinear: a quarrel in Act I between the Caravajal brothers and Benavides seems to announce a subplot, but is quickly resolved. These brothers were however to reappear in the sequel, entitled *The Two Caravajals,* which Tirso promised, and it is possible that the apparent defects of structure in the first half might have seemed less marked when the two parts were taken together. (The moral teaching would also have been reinforced by the story of Fernando's execution of the Caravajals and their challenge to him to meet them before the judgment seat of God.)

The structural weakness of the existing play is compensated for by the evocation of the mood of medieval Spain, with its urge to nationhood struggling through its warring factions, and by an excellent use of foils and contrasts. From the opening *octavas* the two selfish Castilian princes are set against Don Diego, a nobleman from the remote Basque provinces who nevertheless loves the queen and defends her son's claim to his throne; his loyal devotion throughout the play balances their treachery. His description of the rocky Basque country, with its mineral wealth, its tough inhabitants, and its independent spirit symbolized by the famous tree of Guernica, illustrates the author's sense of geography as well as of history, and his respect for the sturdy individualism of that province (905–6).

There is an even stronger contrast between masculine power and ambition and the apparent helplessness of a woman and child. Tirso plays unashamedly on the sentiment evoked by the latter. There is pathos in the child-king's appeal to his mother to lift him down from the throne and take the heavy crown from his head (909a); in the revelation of the persecuted royal pair hiding in the trunk of a tree (914a); and in the queen's baring of her beautiful head as she yields up her widow's wimple, the symbol of matronly modesty and the last of her prized possessions, in order to raise funds for the exchequer. These scenes all make good theater; yet the suggestion of innocent impotence is misleading, for the queen is in fact very strong. In every clash she is more than a match for the wicked princes. Benavides calls her the Spanish Semiramis (914b), and her appearance at the end of each of the first two acts in the emotive guise of a warrior woman, wearing a breastplate and brandishing a sword, belies her apparent helplessness.

What is the source of María's strength? Despite the title of the play it is difficult to attribute it to her prudence, since this is not particularly in evidence. She is prudent in the same way as Don Sancho de Urrea, that is, slow to take revenge; but whether this is wise in her case is another matter, since Don Juan repeatedly treats her clemency as weakness and thinks up a new plot. If she does each time get the better of him it is chiefly through a happy knack of being there at the crucial moment to expose him.[4] Tirso makes repeated use in this play of the theatrical device of the "discovery," the drawing aside of the rear curtain for some unexpected revelation, and more than once it is to disclose the presence of the queen at a strategic moment. She herself gives Don Juan the explanation of her omnipresence: it is because a king has two guardian angels who keep him apprised of any threat of treachery (927a).

This is the real cause of the queen's triumph: neither prudence nor chance, but supernatural power. She is the protector of a king, the chosen of God, and as such she herself has religious overtones. D. W. Moir states that she can be seen as an analogue of the Virgin Mary;[5] and numerous details bear this out. Her name is María, and she is, if not a virgin, at least a chaste widow. Her portrait has miraculous powers, since it falls from the wall at the crucial moment to prevent a treacherous Jewish doctor from poisoning the king. She is the mother of an infant son who is poor and persecuted, yet a king; she likens him to a lamb (907b), and he himself speaks of fleeing from Herod (914b). The repeated "discoveries" have the effect of religious tableaux, particularly the first, the iconlike revelation of the child-king crowned and enthroned.

María is on one level a historical queen; on another, armed like Semiramis, she incarnates a Spain fighting for national identity; on yet another she suggests the Blessed Virgin, and through her the archetypal figure of the chaste mother-goddess. It is clear why she can be involved in no love intrigue; and why, too, the play has such a strong appeal in a country which venerates motherhood and the Virgin Mary as Spain does. Its relevance for the 1620s, and its general advocacy of clemency and prudence, are both subsumed in its patriotic, religious, and archetypal significance.

IV Antona García

A number of other monarchs figure in Tirso's theater, not always in relation with ministers or *privados*. Those occupying the forefront of the action, like María de Molina, are rare. More frequent are background figures like the Portuguese king Manuel, who in *Love Turned Doctor* serves merely to establish the epoch and to give the measure of Jerónima's astonishing success. His predecessor on the Portuguese throne, John II, has a slightly more important role in *The Galician Mari-Hernández;* but although his harsh suppression of the nobility is hinted at, one has only to compare this play with Lope's somber picture of the same king's reign in his tragedy *The Duke of Viseu* to see that Tirso in this instance was not very interested in historical persons or events.

He did not scruple to take liberties with history when he chose. In the course of the discussion in *The Country Houses of Toledo* which follows the performance of *The Shy Man at Court*, a "historian-pedant" accuses him of having invented a fanciful career for a Portuguese prince whose life in reality was very different. Tirso exclaims in self-defense: "As if the license of Apollo should limit itself to historical recollections, and should not be able to build on foundations of real people fictional architectures of the mind!" (I, 141). At the time of writing these words, in 1620 or 1621, he clearly set more store by his own powers of invention than by history.

Thoroughgoing historical drama is in any case rare in Spain. Plays like *Prudence in Woman* and *The Duke of Viseu* are the exception, and there is nothing in the Golden Age to correspond to the grand conspectus of Shakespeare's histories. Spain did however develop a slightly different type of play, one which has firm historical roots and presents kings and queens in important roles, though the main action concerns humbler people. Perhaps the best-known example of this semihistorical type of drama is Lope de Vega's *Fuenteovejuna*. Tirso makes a contribution to the genre with *Antona García*, which is set in the same period.

The monarch in this case is Queen Isabella of Castile, whose marriage in 1469 to Ferdinand of Aragon signaled the virtual unification of Spain after the long unrest of the Middle Ages. Her right to the throne of Castile was not undisputed, and her reign began with a war, the so-called War of La Beltraneja, in which the rival claimant was supported by the Portuguese. In the course of the fighting Portuguese troops occupied the town of Toro with the consent of its overlord, but the populace remained pro-Castilian. A peasant woman, Antona García, conspired with others to plan a revolt, which was unsuccessful and led to their execution; but shortly afterward a shepherd was able to show the besieging Castilians a hidden way up the steep cliffs and into the city, which then fell to Ferdinand and Isabella.[6]

Tirso fuses these two episodes, making the shepherd his *gracioso* and Antona the heroine of a successful assault. On the basis of her enterprise he enlarges her into a figure of almost superhuman vitality; and though an early scene depicts her wedding to the peasant who was historically her husband, he gives her another suitor in the person of the Portuguese count of Penamacor who is fighting on the other side. The substance of the play is therefore roughly half history and half romantic invention.

The license of Apollo does not always stand Tirso in good stead, and here the fanciful material is undoubtedly the weaker part of the play. The count's wooing of Antona reproduces the stock situation of a lovesick nobleman vis-à-vis a sparkling country lass; the quickfire exchanges between them as she sits spinning and he tries to seize her hand are, for all their liveliness, a commonplace of Tirso's theater. Even before her first appearance Antona has been described as a prodigy of both beauty and strength. Her vitality dominates the play, but slides into the grotesque when she picks up a bench and drives some Portuguese travelers out of an inn, only minutes before making two hasty and temporary exits from the stage in order to give birth to twin girls. In making his dazzling heroine so much larger than life Tirso has allowed her to become a freak.

The Antona of the historical action is a more truly heroic figure. Her finest hour comes early in Act II, in a crowd scene that, for sheer theatricality and insight into mob psychology, rivals that of *Julius Caesar*. Juan de Ulloa, overlord of Toro, tries by reasoned discourse to win his people to the Portuguese cause, appealing to them to trust his better judgment. When he fails, his wife María Sarmiento sweeps him aside and harangues them with rhetoric, extracting at last a grudging consent. Then comes Antona. Claiming, like Mark Antony, to be no orator, and scoffing at the logic and the learning of her betters, she plays on the patriotism and instinctive good sense of the people, and soon has them arming themselves with spades, pitchforks, and ploughshares to fight for Isabella and Castile. She herself is wounded in the revolt, and her husband killed; and her reaction to his death, transmuting her silent grief into an even stronger determination to oust the Portuguese, again lifts her to heroic heights.[7]

Historically the siege of Toro was remarkable for the part played in it by women: Isabella was with the Castilian army while Ferdinand fought elsewhere; Antona led her conspiracy; and although Juan de Ulloa was the real power in Toro, his widow María Sarmiento continued to defend the Alcázar after his death. Tirso could hardly fail to rise to the challenge of these warlike women, and playing down their male counterparts he constructs his drama around the three. Moreover, each has a political significance beyond her personal role: the defeat of María, and the close personal bond that grows up between the peasant heroine and her queen, symbolize the social changes of the period, in which feudalism was beginning to collapse and the nobility to lose its power as a major military and political force. *Antona García* is a monarchist play, and the main reason for the exaltation of its heroine is that by analogy the queen is exalted too. There is a strong affinity between them: both, like María de Molina, are compared to Semiramis; both are beautiful, brave, and patriotic; and what Antona is for Toro, Isabella is for Spain.

The play is most often mentioned in connection with the personal references in Act III, where Tirso, speaking in the guise of a traveler in the inn, talks of his envious enemies and his flight from Madrid

(III, 437–39; see p. 26 above). This passage must have been inserted in 1625, the main text probably dating from a year or two earlier, when a lawsuit involving Antona's descendants had drawn attention to her story. This autobiographical relevance should not, however, be allowed to obscure the intrinsic interest of a play which, achieving in its best scenes a genuine re-creation of history in dramatic terms, recalled to a nation in decline that well-loved monarch who symbolized above all other its onetime greatness and strength.

CHAPTER 8

Saints and Sinners

THE Spanish Golden Age theater developed without a break from medieval drama, which had its roots in the church, and it retained an interest in religious material which was largely absent from the contemporary theaters of England and France. Although very few dramatic texts survive from the Middle Ages the sixteenth century saw the development, partly under the influence of the earlier French "miracles," of the *comedia de santo*, or saint play. This dramatized the career of a particular saint, stressing his exemplary qualities and relying heavily for dramatic incident on the miracles associated with his name. But since it usually celebrated the feast day of the saint concerned, which would be as much a holiday as a holy day, it was also a work of entertainment. The major Golden Age dramatists all wrote saint plays, setting their religious material within the usual framework of the Lopean drama, with stock types, *gracioso* humor, love interest, and all the familiar conventions of the secular theater.

I *Tirso's Early Saint Plays*

Karl Vossler believes that it was through the writing of saint plays for schools and monasteries that Tirso first came to the stage.[1] Blanca de los Ríos thinks so too (I, 182a); and they may well be right. Certainly a number of examples are to be found among his early works: *La peña de Francia* (*The Rock of France*), which tells how a simpleminded Frenchman is led to discover a statue of the Virgin in a cleft of a hillside near Salamanca, must antedate *The Shy Man at Court,* since it presents the same rustic couple, Tirso (or Tarso) and Melisa, at an earlier stage in their relationship; *La elección por la virtud* (*Elected for his Virtue*), an account of the rise to eminence of Pope Sixtus V, was one of the plays sold to an acting company in

1612; and the three *Santa Juana* plays can be seen from the extant manuscripts to have been written by 1614.

These plays are all based on earlier hagiographical writings,[2] and perpetuate the tradition of simple medieval piety to which the latter belong. Their protagonists are unwaveringly single-minded. Juana has shown signs of sanctity from her infancy, when she would refuse the breast on a Friday, and now in her teens is aware of a vocation to chastity. The Frenchman Simón Vela shares her aversion to marriage because of his devotion to the Virgin. Félix, the future Sixtus, is a secret aspirant to the priesthood; when he and his sister take their wares to market he leaves her in charge of the stall and slips away to study at the university.

In each case a predisposition to holiness is confirmed, and the future saint set on course, by one or more miraculous revelations. Simón hears a voice telling him to seek out the rock where his true Bride dwells. Juana's wedding dress mysteriously turns into a Franciscan habit. Félix receives repeated indications—a prophecy, a voice, a vision, the discovery of a papal tiara—that he is destined to be pope. The way is never an easy one; Simón has to trudge across two countries to find his rock, and Félix and Juana are both victimized by jealous companions. Yet supernatural favor is always at hand: votes cast against Félix turn out, when read, to recommend him for high office; Juana, excluded from convent worship and given the menial task of doorkeeper, is rewarded by the appearance of the infant Jesus in the revolving hatch. Maurel has counted no fewer than eighteen supernatural interventions in the first part of the *Santa Juana*, nineteen in the second, and twelve in the third.[3] It is undoubtedly this element, rather than any deeper spirituality or moral teaching, that provides the *raison d'être* of Tirso's early saint plays.

Their subplots meanwhile afford the opportunity for love interest and other elements of dramatic convention. *The Rock of France* is one of the plays incorporating historical figures as secondary characters, though in this case their stories are heavily romanticized. Simón Vela stumbles into the political intrigues of the reign of John II of Castile and his troubled relations with his cousins the princes of Aragon. Historically the king's sister was persuaded into a marriage with Prince Enrique for reasons of state; Tirso turns this royal couple into secret lovers, forced by treachery into plotting and pretence. When Enrique, fleeing from prison, adopts the name of Mireno, meets a peasant girl and is taken on as charcoal burner by her father (who will later prove to be an Aragonese count), the links with the comedy of intrigue are plain to see. Félix's rise to greatness is paralleled by his sister's love affair and marriage with a nobleman. These two achieve dignity when faced with parental opposition to an unequal match, but the lighthearted beginnings of their love and their typical quickfire flirtation scene in the market are the stuff of comedy.

II *The* Comendador *Plays*

In *The Rock of France* and *Elected for his Virtue* the role of evil is a relatively minor one. By Part II of the *Santa Juana* trilogy Tirso is focussing more sharply on the contrast between saint and sinner, opposing the virginal Juana's state of grace to the undisciplined lust of the *Comendador* Don Jorge.

It was Lope de Vega who in *Fuenteovejuna* and *Peribáñez* set the pattern for the type of play in which a lord of the manor, who is often a *comendador*, a knight-commander of one of the orders of chivalry, thinks he is free to indulge himself with the girls of the village, resorting to violence if necessary. Lope is chiefly interested in the question of honor, seen in these plays not as the prerogative of birth but as the right of even the humblest individuals to their natural human dignity. In his two great dramas the girls resist, and the knights pay for their dishonorable behavior by death. Tirso takes over the dramatic situation but puts it to a different use.

Don Jorge, a nephew of the Emperor Charles V, no less, abducts Mari-Pascuala from a christening party where she is a godmother; this suggestion of the profanation of a sacrament makes his sin the greater. But she had previously flirted with him and encouraged him. There is very little question of honor, only of human frailty on both sides; and the answer to this is neither dignity nor vengeance, but divine grace. Mari-Pascuala is rescued and taken to Juana's convent. She leaves, falls again, is deserted by Jorge, and thinks of suicide, but Juana appears aloft, in a *tramoya*, to bring her to repentance. Jorge too is converted by an apparition of the saint, who reminds him in the words of a well-known devotional verse of the time of the long account of his life he will one day be called to render (I, 727a).[4] Jorge dies, not at the hands of the wronged villagers but simply through consciousness of the burden of his past life; and what matters most is that his soul is saved.

The subplot of Part III of the trilogy shows another young libertine being brought to repentance through the miraculous intervention of Juana; and the possibilities of the theme are still not exhausted, for Tirso takes it up again on his return from the West Indies, in *La dama del olivar* (*The Lady of the Olive Grove*). This play celebrates the Mercedarian order and was written for its quatercentenary in 1618. It shows clearly the influence of *Fuenteovejuna*, since the abducted girl, Laurencia, has the same name as Lope's heroine and rouses the men of the village to action in a tirade demonstrably based on that of her namesake.[5]

These are far from being the only derivative features of *The Lady of the Olive Grove*, which is a ragbag of familiar elements, both serious and comic, pieced together with astonishing incongruity. The gentle Maroto—neatly characterized in the opening scene when he tells how he has decorated the church with flowers for a feast of Our Lady—shuns marriage, and discovers a statue of the Virgin. She instructs him that a Mercedarian monastery is to be founded on that spot; and when friends disbelieve him she obligingly turns his head round back to front as a confirmatory sign. Laurencia spars flirtatiously with Don Guillén, is abducted and raped by him and then discarded; whereupon she takes to the woods as leader of a robber band, thus effecting a link with another important Golden Age tradition, that of the bandit play. Maroto praises country life in an eloquent paraphrase of Horace's *Beatus ille* ode (I, 1075b); moments later he is reacting to the threat of death from Laurencia's bandits in comic language indistinguishable from that of the *gracioso*. Laurencia's father catalogs her physical charms in a list that includes *culto* comparison of her hair with the sun and her white limbs with the crystal of a river; realistic description of her hands calloused with housework; and some graphic bits of downright bawdy (1047b–48a). Act III moves to and fro between apparitions of the Virgin and scatological humor arising from the *gracioso*'s having been given a purge; his hasty exits are every bit as disconcerting, in their context, as those of Antona García.

The Lady of the Olive Grove is a play that might be better forgotten, except as an example of Tirso's extraordinary lack of touch on occasion, were it not for its very powerful treatment of the *comen-*

dador theme. The sexuality of the episode is stressed much more than in Lope's plays, partly by means of vivid imagery. Maroto in a fine allusive speech likens Laurencia to a hive whose honey has been stolen (1062); the *gracioso* sees her as his master's cast-off shoe, or his horse, whom he himself now proposes to ride bareback (1068a). The climax to this line of the action comes in the abduction scene, when Don Guillén with breathtaking effrontery snatches Laurencia from the presence of Doña Petronila to whom he is betrothed, insulting the latter still further by the blatant sexual imagery of the speech he spits out at her (1066).

He later repents and marries Petronila, while Laurencia is won over to the religious life through the sweet influence of the Virgin, whose command to build the monastery all now accept. Tirso has used some strange material with which to do honor to his order and its patron.

III Quien no cae no se levanta (Who Never Falls Never Rises)

The title of this work indicates an important distinction between it and the early saint plays: this time the protagonist undergoes a change. This is not a contrast between the piety of one simple creature and the sinfulness of others, but the story of a conversion; the sinner herself becomes a saint.

She is an Italian girl, Margarita, and seems to recall the Margaret of Cortona whose religious cult became popular in 1623; though there may have been other models too.[6] For a year she has been Valerio's mistress, and she is now being courted by the married Lelio. But heaven intervenes with a series of warnings. First comes a voice, and visions of the primrose path and the narrow way; these induce a short-lived repentance. Then she hears a sermon preached by St. Dominic, which so moves her that she tears off all her finery and lives soberly for a year. Tempted again by Lelio she is on the point of submitting, but each time she tries to follow him she stumbles and falls. Her guardian angel then appears, enraptures her with his beauty, and carries her to heaven in his embrace.

As in *The Lady of the Olive Grove*, the representation of sin is the liveliest element in this play: Lelio incredibly tearing his wife's jewels from her in order to give them to Margarita, and knocking down her old uncle who tries to intervene (III, 861–63); Margarita stating with shocking frankness that she has known bachelors, now she will get to know the taste of a married man (866a). The penitent

Margarita is insipid by comparison, and her love scene with the angel cloyingly sweet. The Devil, as usual, has all the best lines.

Yet there may be more human truth behind the stages of her conversion than at first appears. The words of St. Dominic reinforce those of the mysterious voice, but still only speak to her conscious mind, so that she rejects her lower nature, symbolized by the clothes and adornments she discards, and gives herself up to mental activity such as insistent reciting of the rosary. Only to the angel can she respond with her whole being. The anonymous editors who continued the publication of the *Obras dramáticas completas* after the death of Blanca de los Ríos object in their preface to this play (III, 845b) that Tirso cheats Margarita, giving the divine messenger a physical attractiveness to which she cannot help but respond, and so exploiting her weakness as a means of luring her to heaven. But the fact is that until her sexuality itself is won over and dedicated to God her conversion cannot be complete. The eroticism of her scene with the angel stands for the sanctification of that part of human nature which is elsewhere so persistently equated with sin.

IV La mujer que manda en casa
(The Wife who Rules the Roost)

Two works of Tirso's mature period that do not belong to the genre of the saint play nevertheless present marked contrasts between sin and righteousness. Each takes its material from the Bible.

The wife who rules the roost is Jezebel, and Tirso draws on 1 Kings 17–21 for the story of Elijah's opposition to Ahab and Jezebel, his sojourn in the desert, the contest with the prophets of Baal, and the episode of Naboth's vineyard. One chapter of the Bible had sufficed for *Tamar's Vengeance*, and it can be argued that there is too much material here. The role of Jezebel's adversary is taken up in turn by Elijah, Naboth, Obadiah, Naboth's wife, and Jehu. Lope de Vega, who did not share Tirso's tendency to overload his plays, would almost certainly have concentrated on either Naboth or Elijah. Tirso makes rather more of Naboth, and from the point of view of structure and action Elijah seems almost expendable; especially since the magnificently dramatic contest with the prophets of Baal, so well narrated in 1 Kings 18 and so splendidly dramatized in musical terms in Mendelssohn's *Elijah*, is not presented on the stage but merely reported.[7] Elijah has another function, however, as will later be shown.

There is biblical warrant for Jezebel's domination of her husband Ahab, and Tirso was obviously attracted by the idea of another strong queen. She is again a Semiramis, and is first seen taking part in the warfare of the chase (I, 450). But her authority is directed to evil ends, and the troubles of Israel are shown to be due to the weakness of a king who is under his wife's thumb. Tirso stresses the point by inventing a character to act as foil to Jezebel: Naboth is given a wife, Raquel, who is gentle and submissive as long as her husband is alive, and only after his death rivals the queen in dramatic stature. The gradual crescendo of Raquel's feelings, from wifely affection through apprehension, jealousy, terror, and grief to vengeful wrath, matches the increasing tension of the play.

The other modification of the biblical account is equally a masterstroke; it is to make Jezebel attempt to seduce Naboth. In this way Ahab's desire for Naboth's vineyard is paralleled by Jezebel's desire for the man himself, and the two major antagonists are brought into a closer confrontation. Naboth is also given a stronger motive for resistance than in the Bible story, where he may seem to a modern reader to react with excessive indignation to Ahab's apparently reasonable offer of a replacement vineyard or a fair purchase price.

But the chief function of Jezebel's lust is to link her with the worship of Baal, and thus with the deeper conflicts that underlie the personal antagonisms of the play. The Bible records that Jezebel was a pagan princess who persuaded her Jewish husband to encourage the worship of a false god; but apart from saying that Ahab made a grove, it gives no indication of the nature of the Baal cult. It was not a question of merely exchanging one god for another, but of a completely different concept of religion. At the time of Ahab and Elijah, as through so much of Old Testament history, the Jewish people was struggling away from a primitive nature religion toward its prophets' vision of a God of the spirit; Jezebel tried to drag it back.

Tirso has understood that Baal worship is a fertility cult, and makes Jezebel an advocate of licentious promiscuity (455). She is placed in luxuriant settings, in the woods and groves of Baal and the lush palace garden where she tries to woo Naboth. Her opponents also have their symbolic backgrounds: Naboth belongs to his vineyard, and Elijah to the desert. Elijah's real significance in the play now begins to be apparent: he is the prophet of the true religion, and represents in particular one strain of it, the ascetic. Naboth, in contrast, leads a normal life in the community; he has a wife, and a vineyard which is his livelihood as well as his patrimony. His way of life is equally in accordance with God's law, but it is a different way from that of Elijah. For Naboth, just as for Lope's Peribáñez, religion is bound up with family life and the cultivation of the land.

The warning against dominant wives seems strangely petty against this striking dramatic presentation of three modes of religion. The primitive and permissive cult of nature is to be abhorred, but for the godfearing Jew—and by extension Christian—two ways are open, the way of total dedication and the way of greater human fulfillment in the life and work of the community. The latter is not a guarantee of happiness or ease: it is Naboth, not Elijah, who has to die for his beliefs.

The play is for the most part a worthy vehicle for these concepts. Convention is relied on only for Jezebel's pretence of talking in her sleep to declare her love to Naboth, and for the interludes of peasant humor. The courtly Italianate meters are extensively used, and despite a satirical aside about *culto* poets that helps to confirm a late date for the play (472a), Tirso more than once in his own imagery shows himself a disciple of Góngora (468b, 486a). More truly poetic than his stereotyped metaphors is a series of conceits relating to the stones with which Naboth is done to death. Stones can be used to build as well as to kill, and these, he tells Jezebel, will raise immortal temples (478b). After the deed is done the "discovery" of Naboth's body amid the bloodstained stones suggests to Raquel a sacrificial offering on a stone altar; and the red blood transmutes them for her into precious stones, rubies for his diadem (482a). Naboth is much more than a victim of palace intrigue: through the symbolism of these stones he becomes a martyr of the church, even a prefiguration of Christ, whose sacrificial death wins him a crown of glory.

V Tanto es lo de más como lo de menos
(Enough is as Good as a Feast)

It has been plausibly suggested that this play is a later version of *Saber guardar su hacienda* (*Looking After One's Property*); this was one of the works sold to an acting company in 1612, but no text has survived under that title (see note 11 to Chapter 2). Professor Kennedy points to echoes of the 1620s in the extant version and thinks there may in fact have been more than one revision. As the play is unique among Tirso's full-length works in being allegorical, she suggests that in its earliest form it may have been an *auto sacramental*.[8] Professor J. C. J. Metford sees evidence that the play was, again most unusually, performed in Lent, and thinks that the date may have been March 1623, when Madrid was suddenly required to entertain the Prince of Wales; secular performances were inappropriate during Lent, but Tirso might well have written or recast a religious work for the purpose.[9]

Its allegorical nature follows from the fact that it is based on two stories that are themselves allegories, the New Testament parables of the Prodigal Son, and Lazarus and the Rich Glutton. It adheres closely to the biblical text of each, in Luke 15 and 16 respectively. Between these two parables in Luke comes that of the Unjust Steward, and this also suggests one scene to Tirso (I, 987–88); though the detail is rather that of the slightly different story in Matthew 18, where a dishonest servant is told by his master to sell his wife and children into slavery to pay off his debt.

All these stories are skillfully linked together in the play, chiefly by means of a newly invented character, the heroine Felicia. She is sought in marriage by three men, the wealthy Nineucio, his nephew Lázaro (Lazarus), and the prodigal Liberio. She chooses Nineucio, but comes to regret the choice when he neglects her in favor of the pleasures of the table. The rejected Liberio meanwhile angrily demands his inheritance and goes off to waste it in riotous living; and Lázaro, equally prodigal in a different direction, impoverishes himself by giving to the poor. After Nineucio's death Felicia marries Liberio, now repentant; and the action extends beyond the grave to show Nineucio in hell and Lázaro in Abraham's bosom, in a final "transformation" scene not unlike that of a typical *auto sacramental*.

The dramatic fabric of interwoven parables is made still firmer by the establishment of new relationships to point parallels and contrasts. Lázaro, who in the Bible is never anything but a beggar at the rich man's gate, in the play is his nephew and a man of some substance, and only becomes poor because of his charity to the same suppliants whom Nineucio has driven away. Liberio's destitution is emphasized by his having to beg for the job of swineherd from his own former servant, the *gracioso* Gulín, who has found favor with Nineucio because his name suggests gluttony.

The introduction of Felicia does not merely unify the plot, it also reinforces the allegory. Her name identifies her as happiness, which all men seek. At first she partners wealth; but though the rich man has the wherewithal to buy her, his self-indulgence has made him impotent to enjoy her. While he is still alive she offers herself to Liberio, but he is by then sufficiently chastened to reject the worldly temptations of a happiness still allied to riches. Only when Nineucio is dead and Liberio has penitently returned home does his father, significantly named Clemente, bestow her upon him. Happiness is not to be sought but comes from a right relationship with a forgiving Father.

Just as the parables themselves are blended, so there is an equally clever blend of allegory with lifelike representation. Apart from some scatological humor on the part of the *gracioso* the usual conventions are dispensed with, and it is paradoxically in this play, based on the unreal characters of moral exempla, that some of Tirso's most realistic dramatization is to be found. Liberio's demanding of his inheritance is superbly rendered, with vigorous dialogue and a clear delineation of the very different characters of the father and the two sons. Most of Act II is devoted to Liberio's wasting of his substance and subsequent disillusionment, and here too the lively scenes of gambling and harlotry are far more convincing than much that passes in Tirso's theater for a representation of real life.

There is a rich use of metaphor in the reflective soliloquies of the destitute Liberio (1014, 1016, 1017), and in the sustained conceit of the swollen river bursting its banks which is repeatedly applied to the rebellious young man (982a, 987a, 1023b). Professor Asensio points to a symbolic quality in the rain which drenches Liberio after he has been stripped by ruffians, and which can be interpreted as a cleansing and regenerative force, a kind of baptism.[10] The same may be said of the fire that destroys his house; his purgation by fire and water is the prerequisite for his repentance.

The play combines some familiar patterns of sanctity and sinfulness: the monochrome protagonists of the early saint plays have their more interesting counterpart in Lázaro; Margarita's conversion is paralleled, more realistically, by that of Liberio. But only Jezebel offers any analogue for Nineucio, and even she behaves as she does because she believes in something. Tirso makes Nineucio a total disbeliever; but goes on to show how his hedonism leaves him little better than dead. One of the great moments of the play is the dying

Lázaro's imprecation to Nineucio who has refused him alms: "I am dying in order to live, but you, whom a different end awaits, will die in order to go on dying, living eternally in your death" (1021a).

At the beginning of the work Nineucio had bragged to Felicia about his great wealth, the favor shown him by the "royal planet" (the king?), and his enjoyment of almost godlike power (978a); Professor Metford sees in these and other details an identification of Nineucio with Olivares. Miss Kennedy agrees that there is political satire in this play, as also in *The Woman who Rules the Roost*, and promises a full study of the subject. The primary model for Nineucio was of course the rich man of the parable, and the slothful and impotent glutton whom Tirso depicts is certainly not in all respects a likeness of the *privado*, who did not lack energy or sexual drive; but it is quite possible that in recasting his work in the 1620s Tirso saw an opportunity to attack the man he had grown to hate, and that the details pointing the analogy were introduced at that stage.

Professor Asensio draws attention to the title. It was a proverbial saying counseling moderation, and Asensio argues that this is in fact what the play is about. Illuminating as his general analysis of the work is, I do not feel that he has quite proved this particular point. He suggests that the closing speech, which inexplicably offers Lázaro as an example of moderation, was added in the process of revision, and that it was really the repentant Liberio who was meant to point the middle way. It seems to me more likely that in refashioning his earlier work Tirso changed both closing speech and title, in order to stress a moral lesson that had not previously been there. This lesson of moderation is linked elsewhere in his theater to the theme of *privanza*: *The Reluctant Favorite* and *Prudence in Woman* both praise the simple life and warn against servants of the state becoming too rich, and the inappropriate title of *Enough is as Good as a Feast* probably represents a further attempt on his part to give a political resonance to the religious work he was recasting.

In this play, as in his presentations of Jezebel and Tamar, Tirso has been faithful to his biblical source and has shown a sure touch for the drama it contains. His additions to the Bible stories are for the most part judicious, and help to bring out the full implications, for his own and subsequent ages, of their simple pictures of good and evil.

CHAPTER 9

Salvation and Damnation

I *The Two Eschatological Dramas*

INSOFAR as the name of Tirso de Molina is known outside Hispanic circles it is usually as the creator of Don Juan: not any of the Don Juans so far encountered in the course of this study, but the internationally famous figure of the great lover. Yet this claim to fame rests on insecure foundations. In the first place, although it is in *El burlador de Sevilla* (*The Trickster of Seville*) that Don Juan Tenorio first acquires a name and a fully elaborated story, he already had a shadowy existence in medieval legends and ballads. Secondly it is not altogether certain that *The Trickster of Seville* is by Tirso. Thirdly the Don Juan it portrays is not a great lover, and the play is not about love, but about trickery and the wages of sin.

The play opens at the court of Naples, where Don Juan has just tricked the Duchess Isabela into the loss of her honor by pretending to be her betrothed, the Duke Octavio. When his crime is discovered his uncle, the Castilian ambassador, reproaches him but helps him to escape, and he sails for Spain. Shipwrecked on the shore near Tarragona he is befriended by a fishergirl, Tisbea, whom he seduces with a false promise of marriage and immediately deserts. He goes to his home town, Seville, where his friend the Marqués de la Mota unwisely mentions his plans for a nocturnal meeting with his beloved, Doña Ana. Don Juan attempts to forestall him, but Ana discovers the impersonation in time; her screams arouse her father, Don Gonzalo, who draws his sword against the trickster and is killed by him.

Don Juan flees from Seville and comes to a village where a wedding is in progress. In the most audacious of his escapades he entices the bride away from her husband on her wedding night, by promising her wealth and noble status. She follows him back to Seville, fondly believing herself to be his wife; meanwhile Tisbea and Isabela have also made their way there in pursuit of Don Juan and their lost honor. The king (Alfonso XI of Castile) has decreed that he must marry Isabela, which he has agreed to do. But at this point a still higher power takes control, with the intervention of the supernatural. Don Juan taunts the statue of Don Gonzalo which has been raised above his tomb and invites it to sup with him; to his astonishment and horror the stone guest turns up at his house, and issues a return invitation which he promises to accept. When he keeps his word and goes to the chapel the statue grasps his hand and, ignoring his plea for a last-minute confession, drags him down into the flames of hell.

This brief summary may give an impression of some structural weakness. It is true that much of the action is episodic, with Don Juan outwitting no fewer than four women in succession, and that the sudden irruption of a supernatural element seems to change the mode of the play. Yet there is no monotony in the episodes, which are diversified by differences in the settings, the circumstances and the characters of the victims, and are accompanied by a gradual thickening of the plot as the wronged women and their menfolk converge on Seville. As regards the sudden switch from lighthearted trickery to divine retribution, to see the action in these terms is to see it only through the eyes of Don Juan. Other characters are by no means so oblivious to the consequences of wrongdoing, and he receives repeated warnings, from his father, from Tisbea, and even from his *gracioso*-servant Catalinón, that he will one day be called to account. He tosses them all off with a metaphor drawn from the world of finance: "¡Qué largo me lo fiáis!" ("What long-term credit you give me!"); that is to say, he does not deny the debt but believes that the calling-in date is still a long way off. His catch-phrase is answered by another which is insistently repeated toward the end: "Quien tal hace, que tal pague" ("Who does such things must pay for them").[1] These warnings build up suspense and leave the audience in no doubt that a reckoning is at hand; so that for them the action follows a natural progression without any disconcerting change of mood.[2]

Its concern with the fate of the soul after death is what links *The Trickster of Seville* with another great drama that may perhaps be by Tirso: *El condenado por desconfiado* (*The Man of Little Faith*). The action of this play is almost unrelievedly somber and intense. It opens with the hermit Paulo, who has lived an ascetic life for ten whole years in order to try and ensure his salvation. Now aged thirty, he dreams that he will go to hell after all; and in his anguish lest this should be true he implores God to reveal to him what his end is to be. In so doing he shows his fundamental error: he wants a guarantee of salvation in exchange for his holy life, instead of being willing simply to trust to God's mercy; he is trying to bargain with God. The Devil had so far found him proof against temptation, but now this deficiency in Paulo's faith gives him his chance, and he appears in the guise of an angel pretending to bring the divine revelation that Paulo had sought. His message is that the hermit must go down into the city of Naples where he will meet one Enrico whose end is to be the same as his.

Paulo never doubts that this is the word of God and assumes that Enrico must be a great saint. To his horror he turns out to be a thief, rapist, and murderer who brags of committing innumerable crimes out of the sheer love of evil. If ever anyone was destined for hell it would seem to be Enrico, and Paulo therefore despairs of any other end for himself. He abandons his ascetic life and returns to the hills as a murderous brigand; but he takes no delight in wickedness, as Enrico does, and is still obsessed by the damnation that awaits him. A shepherd seeking a lost sheep tries to persuade him to repent and trust in God, but he cannot do this. In a magnificently dramatic confrontation Paulo takes Enrico prisoner, threatens to kill him, and implores him to make a confession first, so as to open the way to heaven for them both. Enrico refuses as yet, but explains that for all his wickedness he still has faith in God's mercy; the sinner preaches to the former saint. Even then Paulo cannot trust God.

Despite his record Enrico has one saving grace, his love for his old father Anareto, whom he supports out of the proceeds of his crimes. This one virtue is literally his salvation, since it is only in answer to Anareto's pleas that he does finally agree to make the necessary confession. He has been released by Paulo and caught by the police, and is almost prepared to go to his execution unshriven. (His long delay in repenting is necessary to maintain suspense in the audience, who know from the title that Paulo will be damned but must be left in doubt as long as possible about Enrico.) In the end his love for his father prevails, and his soul is seen being borne aloft by angels. When Paulo hears this he believes at last that he too is sure of heaven, and as he dies, in a skirmish with the law, words of hope are on his lips; but a final vision of him lapped in flames makes plain his tragic error.

There can be no doubt about the taut construction of this play. Although there are two main characters there is no duality of plot; almost from the beginning the Devil's prophecy links them together, and they remain foils to each other throughout. Paulo's moral and spiritual degradation is balanced by Enrico's upward struggle to heaven; the rise of the one is the measure of the other's fall.

Prophecy and its fulfillment is a device often used to give shape to a play; *Macbeth* is one of the best-known examples. *The Man of Little Faith* employs it in a subtle and original way. There is not one prophecy but two, Paulo's dream and the Devil's prediction. The dream comes true, as the audience, alerted by the title, expects that it will; but the changing stances of the two protagonists keep the outcome of the second prophecy in doubt until the very end. When it is not fulfilled the break with dramatic tradition serves as a reminder of its diabolical origin. The two prophecies, which sometimes seem to be reinforcing each other and at other times to be in conflict, are a powerful source of tension and suspense.

II Problems of Authorship

It seems peculiarly unfortunate that neither of these major works, which give such superb dramatic expression to the spiritual preoccupations of their day, can be assigned with absolute certainty to any author. The circumstances in which each was published were outlined in Chapter 2 (see p. 39, 40). The arguments for and against Tirso's authorship must now be examined.

Doubts arise about *The Trickster of Seville* because it was not published in any of Tirso's *partes*. The earliest surviving text is in a collection of works by various dramatists dating from 1630; but in default of any other claim the fact that it was there attributed to Tirso offers at least a presumption in favor of his authorship. The question is complicated by the existence of another version of the play, which has as its title Don Juan's catch-phrase ¡*Tan largo me lo fiáis!* (*What Long Credit You Give Me!*); both texts are included by Blanca de los Ríos in Volume II of Tirso's *Obras dramáticas completas*. Most scholars agree that *What Long Credit* is the earlier version, but that both it and the better-known *Trickster* are revi-

Salvation and Damnation

sions of a still earlier original, now lost.[3] At which of these three stages of composition, if any, was Tirso de Molina involved?

There is some evidence to suggest that the original play was by Tirso. A study of *The Trickster* reveals a number of features that are almost commonplaces of his theater: exchanges between young men in which the defects of the local girls are passed in review (II, 654), as occur also in *Tamar's Vengeance* (III, 364–5) and *Who Never Falls* (III, 872); talk of the power of love to unite "seda con sayal" ("silk with coarse wool," 649a), a formula found repeatedly in plays where noblemen woo village girls; the *gracioso*'s scatological jokes (660a, 676a).

These are all incidental touches that could have been added later; and in fact the "seda con sayal" formula is not used in *What Long Credit*, although that is not to say that it was not there in the original. But more strikingly, a number of more integral elements in *The Trickster of Seville* are also to be found in the *Santa Juana* trilogy. Tisbea (II, 650) and Mari-Pascuala (I, 719–20) both bewail their desertion in speeches in octosyllabic ballad meter punctuated by refrains in hendecasyllables; and Mari-Pascuala's refrain "Woe to the woman who trusts in men!" is also uttered by both Tisbea and the Duchess Isabela as they make their way to Seville (II, 672, 673). The libertine Don Luis of *Santa Juana III* receives a warning from a soul in purgatory who grasps his hand; flames spurt from it and Luis exclaims "I'm burning! I'm on fire!" (I, 772b), as does the trickster in his last moments. The warnings to Don Juan and his response in terms of a debt not yet due are paralleled by Juana's reminder to Don Jorge of an account to be rendered and payment to be made forthwith (I, 727b); indeed, financial imagery of this kind is frequent in Tirso's religious dramas.[4] Containing as it does so many recognizably Tirsian elements, spread throughout the play, *The Trickster of Seville* would certainly seem to be fundamentally the work of Tirso de Molina.

On the other hand, one feature that is a constant in Tirso's theater, from the early *Elected for his Virtue* and *Santa Juana* through *The Lady of the Olive Grove* to the late *Mari-Hernández* and *Antona García*, is absent from *The Trickster of Seville* although opportunities for it exist. This is what I have called the quickfire flirtation scene between a nobleman and a peasant girl. One might not expect it in the case of the slow-witted rustic bride Aminta, but Tisbea has much more about her and could certainly have carried it off. Instead she first introduces herself in language that is astonishingly *culto* for a fishergirl (640-42), after which the courtship ritual that follows is much more of a stately minuet than a darting thrust and parry. The carefully worded speeches, with the marked auditory effect of the repeated *-áis* and *-éis* rhymes, have an almost operatic quality quite alien to Tirso, and if there is any whole scene in *The Trickster of Seville* not by him I would suggest that it is this first part of the Tisbea episode (640b-45b); the latter part, after the interruption of the scene in Seville, reads much more like his work (648a-51).

Professor Wade in a recent edition of the play makes out a good case for the intervention at some point of the impresario and minor dramatist Andrés de Claramonte. Some otherwise unimportant textual and bibliographical details suggest that the text of *The Trickster* had passed through Claramonte's hands, and therefore that he may have been the actor-manager who put it on. The 1630 edition states that it was performed by Roque de Figueroa, but this may refer to later productions. Wade thinks that Tirso wrote the original and sold it to Claramonte, who twice doctored it for performance; the first revision produced *What Long Credit* and the second *The Trickster of Seville*. In view of the similarities with *Santa Juana* the original probably dates from Tirso's early period, and both revisions must have been in existence by the time of Claramonte's death in 1626.[5]

The chief drawback to Wade's suggestions is that they presuppose either that the lost original was already a masterpiece—and there is nothing in the works known to date from Tirso's early period to indicate that he was capable at that stage of such sustained dramatic power—or that the undistinguished Claramonte had the ability to make a masterpiece out of it. Daniel Rogers has shown, in the article referred to in note 2 to this chapter, that in so far as *The Trickster* differs from *What Long Credit* the former is the better play, and that the differences nearly all serve to enhance its artistic coherence. They may represent a quality that had been present in the original and was lost from *What Long Credit*, but the more likely inference is that Tirso himself revised and improved his own earlier work; perhaps, as with *The Melancholic*, taking up again in his Madrid period a drama from the previous decade in which he now saw richer possibilities. Until more evidence is forthcoming, however, the precise relationship of the different versions can only remain a matter of supposition.

Salvation and Damnation

The authorship of *The Man of Little Faith* is a still more open question. Its appearance in Tirso's Second *parte*, and the known facts about the paternity of six of the twelve plays in that cryptic volume, leave only a one in six chance that this one is by Tirso; on the other hand no conclusive arguments point to anyone else.

There are two pieces of evidence, one external and one internal, that can be adduced in favor of Tirso's authorship. The first is a jotting discovered by Dr. A. K. G. Paterson in a manuscript of another play, and headed "Primera de Tirso." Paterson believes this to be a list of the plays intended for Tirso's First *parte*, the volume sent to the press in 1624 but not published; the list consists of twelve titles and the last is *The Man of Little Faith*. Since the other eleven are all Tirsian works this would seem to be a strong pointer. On the other hand the manuscript bears the date 1638; not only is this a long time after 1624, but by that date *The Man of Little Faith* had been published in the Second *parte* under Tirso's name, so the list does not necessarily constitute independent evidence.[6]

If we search the play itself for Tirsian trademarks we shall find no familiar details of the kind scattered through *The Trickster of Seville*. The one close analogy with a play by Tirso concerns Paulo's mistaken belief at the beginning that he might be saved through his own merits; this belief is shared by a minor character in *El mayor desengaño* (*The Greatest Disillusion*), a work published in the First *parte* of 1627. This is a saint play about Bruno, founder of the Carthusian order; he achieves sanctity as a result of successive disillusionments, first with love, secondly with *privanza*, and thirdly with learning and scholarship. This last disenchantment comes after the death of the studious and holy Dion, who had prayed to be judged on his own merits; it is revealed that his prayer is answered, and that he is consequently damned.[7] There is a parallel here with Paulo's dream; and the fact that it is very rare in the Golden Age religious theater for any character, however wicked, to be consigned to hell, may suggest that if Tirso could do it in the case of Dion and Don Juan he may also be responsible for Paulo.[8] Yet the risk of eternal damnation was a very common topic in the sermons and manuals of the day, and even this piece of internal evidence can by no means be regarded as conclusive.

Professor Kennedy, who almost certainly knows Tirso's theater and that of his contemporaries better than any other living scholar, believes that *The Man of Little Faith* is not by him.[9] My own feeling is that as regards style and dramatic technique it does not seem like a Tirso play; though as I would have said the same about *Prudence in Woman* this proves nothing. Its authorship must for the present, and perhaps for ever, remain an open question. What is not in doubt is the importance of the play, or the fact that in default of any other substantiated claim room must be found for it in this consideration of Tirso's theater.

III *Sources and Teaching*

Investigations into the sources of the two dramas have revealed the existence of widespread and persistent legends behind each of them: in the case of *The Trickster*, medieval legends and ballads about young braggarts who taunt the dead, perhaps mingled with memories of real-life libertines; in the case of *The Man of Little Faith*, legends from the east about the relative merits of the outwardly holy man and the notorious sinner.[10] Other enquiries have related the latter play to the theological controversies of the sixteenth century, particularly the debates over predestination and free will, and have tried to determine which school of theological thought it follows.

On this question of religious teaching recent critics have tended to look less far afield and to see both plays as simple and orthodox expressions of the lessons being emphasized by the preachers and devotional writers of the day. Blanca de los Ríos recalls the spiritual guides of Louis de Blois, or Ludovicus Blosius, which went through seventeen editions in Spanish translation in the early seventeenth century, and which in places seem clearly to anticipate the cases of Don Juan, Paulo, and Enrico.[11] Serge Maurel produces even more apposite quotations from Blosius to show, not that the two plays were necessarily based on his writings, but that at the time of their appearance the various attitudes toward sin and repentance that they exemplify were very much in the minds of priests and people.[12] Daniel Rogers in his recent edition of *The Man of Little Faith*,[13] which contains much the best study of the play so far, surveys the previous enquiries into its sources and concludes that there is no need to look beyond the New Testament for the substance of its teaching. This can be summed up in a well-known Thomist formula: no one is damned except through his own fault, and no one is saved except through the mercy of God.

The two plays give the impression of being companion pieces by reason of their eschatology, even if they present opposite sides of the coin. Don Juan's damnation is the inevitable result of his actions: "Who does such things must pay for them." Enrico and Paulo illustrate rather the importance of faith: no man, however good, can earn salvation, and no sinner, however depraved, will be damned if he repents and throws himself on God's mercy. Yet even Enrico is not entirely lacking in good deeds, and it is precisely his love for his father that gives him the grace to repent. Faith and works are interlinked in the scheme of salvation.

It is important however to realize that the faith Paulo lacks is not belief in the existence of God and the reckoning to come; these he never doubts. None of the characters in these plays, not even Don Juan, is an atheist like Nineucio. What Paulo is short of is faith in the sense of confidence, trust in God; he thinks that heaven not only can but must be earned, by his own efforts. In *The Trickster of Seville* the reiterated financial terminology, the talk of credit, payment, time-limits, and calling-in, puts salvation on a legalistic and contractual basis. Ironically, this is the way Paulo understands it. He is prepared to be legalistic; he invariably sees God as judge (II, 456a, 469b, 479a), and only asks for a fair trial. But the lesson of his play is not justice but mercy. *The Trickster* gives a stern, Old Testament-type warning about the wages of sin, *The Man of Little Faith* offers the free gift of mercy to the sinner, if he will only ask for it. It is, in Rogers' words, "not so much a warning as an appeal."[14]

Tirso, it will be remembered, exalted mercy over justice in *Tamar's Vengeance*. (This play was probably written in 1623. Rogers thinks 1624–1625 the most likely date for *The Man of Little Faith*, and Miss Kennedy suggests 1622.)[15] *The Man of Little Faith* certainly seems to show a deeper spiritual understanding than the probably earlier *Trickster of Seville*, whether or not they are by the same man. Yet if its lesson is more sublime, the expression of it is in some ways less poetic. *The Man of Little Faith* expounds its teaching through the mouths of the shepherd and of the captive Enrico; *The Trickster* also preaches, in the many warnings given to Don Juan, but it makes its points additionally through the more subtle medium of symbolism.

The action opens at night, *in medias res*, with Don Juan just having seduced Isabela in an assumed identity. She prepares to light a candle to show him out, and he exclaims "I will put out your light!" He needs the dark for his deceptions, and all through the play he is linked with the idea of darkness. His escapades all take place at night, and his tricks and lies spread the darkness of confusion round him. He is an enemy of the light; he puts out the candle that would reveal the truth, just as he extinguishes the light of honor in his victims and the light of Don Gonzalo's life. The village wedding scene opens in the sunshine of an April morning, and Aminta likens her husband Batricio to the sun; the arrival of Don Juan brings gloom, and Batricio thinks it is the Devil, the prince of darkness, who has sent him there (663–64).

It is at night that the trickster comes into his own. "These are my hours," he tells Aminta when she questions his appearance in her room at bedtime (669b); and before each adventure he creates suspense with his impatience for nightfall, calling attention to the setting sun or eagerly laying his plans for "this very night." Yet this urgency about the immediate future is missing from his view of life as a whole, and contrasts with his complacent belief that he has unlimited time ahead. In this way a powerful tension is created between swiftness and slowness, and the passage of time itself acquires symbolic value. His impatience for the night will bring the night of death much sooner than he expects, just as his deeds of darkness will lead to an eternity in the darkness of hell.[16]

IV Enrico and Paulo

Whatever other means a drama uses to make its points it must always use characters, and Enrico and Paulo are both clearly conceived with didactic intention. They are perfect foils for each other, being contrasted in almost every possible way. Paulo is mistrustful, Enrico almost too trusting, delaying his vital confession until the last moment. Enrico is aggressive and violent, Paulo's activity is largely in the mind; even when he has turned bandit he gets Pedrisco to do the robbing and hanging for him. Enrico is an extrovert, at home in the city, and his nature is revealed mainly through his contacts with other people, while Paulo reveals himself in soliloquies and invocations to his natural surroundings. When Paulo decides to emulate Enrico in wickedness he does not copy the latter's urban crimes of gambling, burglary, and arson, but goes back to the countryside as a brigand.

Out of the banditry which constituted a real social problem both in the kingdom of Naples (where the play is set) and in Catalonia in the late sixteenth and early seventeenth centuries, there had grown up a literary tradition of bandit novels and bandit plays. As a rule the protagonists of these are not inherently bad but have suffered some injustice and taken to the wilds as a form of revenge against society. Laurencia of *The Lady of the Olive Grove* is a minor example, and Paulo's sudden impulse belongs to the same literary tradition. Enrico too is in large measure a figure of literary convention, the convention of the sinner on the grand scale who is nevertheless capable of an equally spectacular repentance. Professors Whitby and Anderson have shown that one precedent for Enrico is undoubtedly the Leonido of *La fianza satisfecha* (*A Bond Honored*), many of whose boasts of wickedness are echoed by Enrico in almost identical words.[17]

Enrico's catalog of crime (467-68) is so horrendous that it can hardly be taken at its face value; no one could in reality have got away with so much for so long. There is certainly a strong streak of bravado in Enrico, and though he maintains twice over that every word is true, it must be remembered that he is taking part in a contest to try and prove himself the most wicked of his set. But more important for the understanding of the play is the fact that Paulo is listening, and that what he hears about Enrico must be bad enough to justify his total collapse into despair.

Similarly with Enrico's extreme devotion to his aged father, which it is impossible to reconcile realistically with his other deeds: both the pious old Anareto himself, who has so improbably fathered and nurtured such a monster, and the relationship between the two, must be understood in terms of what the play has to teach. Professor A. A. Parker sees in the father figure a symbol of authority and an analogue of God, and suggests that it is because Enrico retains a right relationship with Anareto that in the end he can be reconciled with his heavenly Father.[18] Mr. Rogers agrees, contrasting Enrico's loving and suffering father with Paulo's angry God. For Professors Whitby and Anderson Anareto stands rather for Enrico's conscience, since he finds it impossible to do wrong in his presence.[19] These interpretations are not mutually exclusive, and all help to show how the play should be approached.

Integral as Enrico is to the work, it is Paulo on whom the title focusses attention and who is the more fully characterized of the two. Few characters in Golden Age drama pass with such rapidity through so many changes of mood. His opening soliloquy expresses delight in nature and joy at having been withdrawn from the wicked world and set on the road to salvation; his gratitude to God is not without a hint of the Pharisee's smugness. This yields to panic after his dream of the judgment in which his good deeds were outweighed by his sins, and he beseeches, even commands God to let him know his fate. The Devil's prophecy brings some reassurance, and he clings nervously to the hope it offers. There is a revealing incident when, as he and Pedrisco make their way into the city, the latter points out the house of a girl whom Paulo had courted before he became a hermit. His reaction is extreme: unclean thoughts and memories of past joys assail him, and he gets Pedrisco to trample on him in order to mortify the flesh; the real nature of his heavy consciousness of guilt begins to be apparent.

The crucial scene for Paulo is one in which he is merely an observer: he listens with growing anguish to Enrico's account of his exploits, and when it is over bursts into tears of black despair. Then comes his impulsive decision to rival Enrico in sin, leading to his one assertive phase. He accepted God as judge, but he had at least expected a fair trial, and a fair trial he will have, even if it means becoming a criminal in order to justify the verdict. All his reasoning is based on the idea of fairness: "It is not right that I should be doing penance and he indulging himself in the city, and that we should then have the same end after death" (470a); "God forgive me if I offend him, but if we are to have the same end this is fair, and I know what I am about" (478a); "when God, the eternal Judge, condemns me to hell, at least I shall have done something to deserve it" (479a). In his revolt against the unfairness of what he thinks has been predicted he stands up to God and tries to force him willy-nilly into the role of *justus Judex*.

But he cannot sustain this mood for long. He was not cut out for violence; his crimes, bad as they are, do not match Enrico's, and he shows nothing of the same gusto in committing them. Despair returns, lifting momentarily when he almost comes to believe the Good Shepherd's message of hope; but his consciousness of guilt proves too strong. And it is almost certainly not his recent crimes of brigandage that weigh him down, but the earlier sins that had tilted the balance in his dream, the temptations of the flesh he had tried so hard to mortify. If it was not enough to have exiled himself to the desert, for ten long years feeding on bitter herbs and drinking brackish water, then he can see no way out.

Yet even if he cannot trust God's mercy he continues to trust implicitly in the prophecy which he believed was the word of God. When in his dying moments he hears of Enrico's heavenward flight, hope, even certainty, returns to him, and the supreme tragic irony is that the mistrustful Paulo dies expecting after all to be saved. His reappearance in flames proclaims the truth. There was no need for self-punishment in the wilderness: all that was needed was to say "God be merciful unto me, a sinner."

Maurel believes that Paulo forfeits sympathy through his "cold and rigorous logic."[20] Parker sees him as a mediocre type, in contrast to Enrico who has the stuff of greatness in him. It seems to me doubtful whether the author intended quite such harsh judgments of Paulo. Despite the tragic error induced by his pathological sense of guilt,[21] one cannot but admire his rocklike resistance over so many years, to which even the Devil pays tribute (456b), and his unwavering faith in what he took to be a divine revelation. And those who retain a belief in human effort and self-discipline must surely feel some sympathy with his outraged sense of justice at the idea that all his striving is to count for nothing.

The view of Paulo closest to the author's intention, however, is almost certainly that of Rogers, who paints an understanding and deeply moving picture of a man paralyzed by largely imagined guilt; a man who, because he cannot accept or love himself, cannot love or hope to be accepted by God; and whose lack of self-confidence, like that of countless others after him, is self-fulfilling. It is men like this whom the dramatist wishes to persuade, or for whom at least he hopes to arouse compassion: "Might a play about the distorted vision of one of them, if only it could be subtle enough, help a few others to see, or at least win a little pity for them? *Mutatis mutandis*, it may do so now."[22]

V Don Juan and his Companions

The story of Don Juan has been frequently retold, and a myth has grown up around his name. He has become the universal lover, the embodiment of sexual energy, the man irresistible to women. In *The Trickster of Seville* he is none of these things. He does not love any of his victims, and makes only the briefest acknowledgments of any physical desire. There is no suggestion that his sexuality is at all abnormal: his friend the Marqués de la Mota is also promiscuous, and in one sense more reprehensibly so, since he frequents the brothels of Seville at the same time as he is paying court to Doña

Ana whom he hopes to marry. Personal attractiveness is not the reason for Don Juan's success, since on two occasions he is pretending to be someone else, and in the case of Aminta he arouses a dislike only overcome by promises of wealth; only between himself and Tisbea does there seem to be any real mutual attraction, and even she has taken the trouble to find out the shipwrecked gentleman's name and status before welcoming him back to consciousness in her arms.[23]

Don Juan's real motivation is indicated in the title: what he seeks each time is not so much sexual enjoyment as the satisfaction of pulling off a *burla*, or trick. The picaresque literature of Golden Age Spain bears witness to the great vogue of the *burla*, which usually contained an element of both clever deception and practical joke. It was obscurely connected with the idea of honor, since to allow oneself to be tricked was to lose face, while the successful trickster gained in esteem. Don Juan is proud of his reputation as a *burlador*: "Trickery is an old habit of mine" (648a); "Seville calls me the Trickster, and my greatest pleasure is to trick a woman and rob her of her honor" (656b). It is significantly the code of honor, with its insistence on feminine purity, that provides him with the necessary stimulus in the form of a challenge to his ingenuity.

The whole play is constructed on the repeated pattern of challenge answered by *burla*. Tisbea is so ready to fall that only the very simple trick of a promise of marriage was required; but Ana, being the beloved of his friend, offers a greater challenge, to which he responds with a "famous trick" (659a): telling the Marqués she was expecting him at twelve o'clock when the message had really said eleven, so as to allow himself time to slip in first. As for the challenge of Aminta, the bride on her wedding day, this requires "the most select trick of all" (668b), and Don Juan pulls it off by cunningly manipulating husband and wife in turn with false notions of honor.

Then it is that he overreaches himself, and not content with acquiring a twisted kind of honor through overcoming challenges, dares to issue one himself. He challenges Don Gonzalo's statue to take its threatened revenge, and in what follows the trickster himself is tricked—always for reader or audience the most satisfying *burla* of all. The statue's deception is cleverly linked with Don Juan's own typical procedures. It appeals to his sense of honor in order to get him to the chapel, and he, who had broken so many airy promises, this time ironically keeps his word. It asks him for his hand—the symbol of good faith—and tells him not to fear; but he, who had so often given his hand to women in bad faith, is this time the dupe, and perishes in the fiery grip.

The whole of Don Juan's career, as well as his final fatal rendezvous, is motivated by his perverted sense of honor. Yet there are other characters in the play whose behavior is less than perfectly honorable: not only the lecherous marquis, but older men in positions of authority of whom more might have been expected. Don Juan's uncle, the ambassador to Naples, scolds his nephew but engineers his escape, even though this means implicating an innocent man. His father, who is the king's *privado*, threatens him with hellfire, but is only too glad to accept the king's arrangements for covering up the disgrace, and can say complacently that "all is turning out well" (679a). The king himself is more concerned with appearances than with the punishment of wrong, and even bestows a title on the trickster in order to make him a suitable husband for the Duchess Isabela.

Neither are the women in the play such innocent victims as to evoke much real sympathy. Isabela and Ana are too ready to anticipate marriage; Aminta cannot help her stupidity, but should have loved her husband more than wealth; Tisbea virtually offers herself to Don Juan. Ana, it is true, had some excuse in that the king had promised her to a man she did not even know, and she wanted to make sure of being married to Mota whom she loved; but in general the picture offered is of a corrupt society in which nearly all place private satisfaction and advantage before moral considerations of right and wrong.

Of the major characters in the work only two command any real admiration. One is the *gracioso* Catalinón, who never ceases to criticize and warn his master, and who utters the play's one word of compassion: when Don Juan chortles over the tricking of Aminta, his comment is: "A neat and amusing trick indeed, but one she will weep for to the end of her days" (673b).[24] The other is Don Gonzalo, a *comendador* and trusted ambassador to Lisbon, who dies nobly trying to prevent Don Juan's escape. He has been doubly wronged by the trickster, and it is therefore fitting that he should take revenge on behalf of all the latter's victims; while his upright life fits him also to be the instrument of divine retribution against the man who insolently dared to challenge the heavenly law.

VI Dramatic Qualities

A didactic intention in a work of literature always raises the question of whether the work still succeeds in purely literary terms. There can be little doubt about the stageworthiness of these two plays. It is true that both do resort to preaching, *The Man of Little Faith* at much greater length than *The Trickster*. But both also make their points through conflicts of character, buildup of suspense, and the specifically dramatic means of staging and stage action.

Mr. Rogers has shown in his edition how well *The Man of Little Faith* exploits the resources of the simple Golden Age stage: the Devil appearing in the upper gallery, recognizable to the audience but unseen by Paulo down below; the "discovery" of the aged Anareto; Paulo's death fall from above, and descent and reemergence through the trapdoor. The action shifts between countryside and town, and in the latter between street and interior, seashore and prison. Scenes of violence resulting from Enrico's aggressions alternate with outwardly quieter passages where the turmoil is all in Paulo's mind. The one scene where the two men meet face to face, when Paulo has Enrico physically at his mercy and yet is agonizingly dependent on his state of mind and soul, offers a superb expression in visual terms of the paradox at the heart of the work.

The Trickster of Seville has even more action, to which Don Juan imparts a sense of pace and urgency all the time he is on the stage. Its settings include two royal palaces, the dark streets of Seville, and the eerie chapel, and, contrasting with these, the sunlit Mediterranean shore and the spring morning of the wedding. Seville itself comes to life with the talk of the Portuguese brothels in Sierpes Street, the torches and hubbub in the courtyard of the Alcázar, and even an advertisement for a local pub (654a); and for sheer theatricality, could any scene match the arrival of the stone guest, or hell let loose in the dark chapel?[25]

Both these masterpieces, whoever their author or authors may be, give powerful expression to the deeper moral and spiritual preoccupations of their day. And it was probably not to individuals only that they spoke. The movements for reform bore witness to the fairly widespread desire for moral regeneration on a national scale, and the warnings of *The Trickster of Seville* may have been intended as a contribution to this. Similarly, J. H. Elliott has shown how Spain had suffered since the beginning of the century from a debilitating sense of desolation: "The unbroken succession of disasters threw Castile off balance. The ideals which had buoyed it up during the long years of struggle were shattered beyond repair. The country felt itself betrayed—betrayed perhaps by a God who had inexplicably withdrawn His favour from His chosen people."[26] If for the succession of disasters we substitute Paulo's shattering dream, this could almost be a description of the hermit's own reactions; and the story of his fate might well have had a message for this mood of national despair. But more significant for the modern student of literature is the fact that both plays speak their lessons in the genuinely dramatic language of the stage.

CHAPTER 10

Other Works

I Autos sacramentales

THE *auto sacramental* was a peculiarly Spanish development of medieval church drama. Like the early Christmas and Easter tropes it celebrated a religious festival, in this case the feast of Corpus Christi. It was part entertainment, part liturgical act, since although performed in the open air as part of the holiday celebrations it always ended with public display and worship of the Host. *Autos* were one-act allegorical pieces comprising three elements: the surface story, which might derive from a biblical or other religious source but could equally well use secular material; the underlying meaning, which would be some moral or doctrinal lesson; and the sacramental ending, to which the story was required to lead up in as natural a manner as possible.

During the seventeenth century the *auto* performances in each town were organized by the local authorities. They commissioned the dramatists of the day to write the texts, and *autos* by Lope, Tirso, and other playwrights survive, as well as the seventy by Calderón who became the master of the genre. Actors were chosen to perform them from among the companies employed in the secular theater. The *auto* thus had close links with the regular drama; it borrowed many of its devices and conventions, including stock types like the *gracioso*, and even some of its actual stories.

Four *autos sacramentales* by Tirso have survived. He himself included three of them in his collection *Deleitar aprovechando* (*Pleasure with Profit*). A fourth, *El laberinto de Creta* (*The Cretan Labyrinth*), exists in a manuscript dated 1638 that bears his name, though it is not in his own hand; it has some typically Tirsian features, particularly in the character and language of the *gracioso*, and there seems no reason to doubt the attribution. A collection of *autos* published in 1664 included one ascribed to Tirso, *La madrina del*

Other Works

cielo (*The Heavenly Sponsor*); whether or not it is by him it is not a sacramental piece, but one written for a feast of the Virgin. The three *autos sacramentales* included in *Pleasure with Profit* will be considered here.

In introducing these three works in his miscellany Tirso states where each one was first performed and by whose company; and by setting this information against the theatrical records of the time it can be deduced that they are all early works, dating from the Toledan period.[1] *El colmenero divino* (*The Divine Beekeeper*) and *Los hermanos parecidos* (*The Identical Brothers*) were both first put on in Toledo itself, and *No le arriendo la ganancia* (*Much good may it do him!*) in Madrid.

The first-named of these *autos* tells how the divine beekeeper comes down from his hilltop dwelling to set up a beehive in the valley. At first the bee is happy in his love and care; but along comes a bear who tempts her with poisoned honey, which turns her black and causes her wings to shrivel. A worldly beekeeper tries to entice her into his hives, but repelled by what she sees there she turns again to her divine master, who feeds her on pure honey and restores her beauty. The transition to the sacramental ending is made easy by a play on the words "panal," honeycomb, and "pan," bread: the true honey is the Bread of Life, containing in itself all sweetness, which is received in the sacrament.

This is thus one of the many *autos* that use a simple rustic motif to convey the vast dogma of the creation, fall, and redemption of mankind. The allegory is perhaps less perfect than it might have been in the hands of Calderón, whose rigorous intellect usually enabled him to achieve exact correspondences in all details between story and meaning. Professor Wardropper points out the oddity of love between a beekeeper and his bee;[2] and the role of the bear, who tempts the bee instead of stealing its honey, is also somewhat forced.

Yet the rusticity has considerable charm, particularly in the lifelike exchanges of the early pages. There is a nice robustness in the corporeal drone's jealous mockery of the soul-bee: "You forever sitting neat and dainty in your parlor, waited on hand and foot, while all the dirty work falls on me" (I, 11). And no allegory could be more ingenious than the opening dialogue between the beekeeper and the *gracioso:* the former tells how he has come down from the town of Mountjoy, where his father is mayor; this peaceful place is a second Jerusalem, and all its inhabitants real angels; the father lives like a king there, and never looks a day older; their friend, as gentle as a dove, is also planning a visit to the valley at Whitsuntide; and so on (6–7). Phrase after phrase succeeds in conveying celestial mysteries in authentic conversational tones.

Tirso records that *The Identical Brothers* was first performed by the Valenciano twins, and the central fact of its story is that Christ becomes man's brother, indistinguishable from him in appearance. Man has been made God's viceroy on earth, but his wife, Vanity, persuades him to eat the forbidden fruit, and his *privado*, Desire, encourages him to gamble his substance away. (A passage on the evils of *privanza*, and referring to the replacement of trustworthy servants, the influence of court jesters, and the outlandishness of modern fashion, has every appearance of having been added in the 1620s [I, 1584b–85b].) Man so mismanages God's earthly kingdom that he is threatened with judgment; but Christ takes his place, unrecognized, and pays the penalty for him. The sacramental ending follows quite naturally as Christ offers His body and blood from the Cross; He Himself becomes the fruit of the Tree of Life, replacing the forbidden fruit of the garden.

This substitution of the sinner by Christ recalls a recurrent medieval legend, in which it is usually an erring nun whose absence from her convent goes unnoticed because the Virgin Mary has taken her place. Tirso uses this expedient, facilitated by the availability of identical twins to act the parts, in order to create another allegory of man's fall and redemption. The price of the ransom, represented by Christ's sufferings, this time receives due attention. Indeed the metaphor of money and payment is sustained through much of the work: gambling debts must be settled and misdeeds paid for; Christ, who has the necessary capital, will act as surety; He will give *barato* (the largesse distributed by successful gamblers) in the form of grace; and He will Himself become the document discharging the debt. The financial imagery, including the twice-repeated formula "Who does such things must pay for them," links this little work with *The Trickster of Seville*, and reinforces the suggestion that that drama too dates originally from Tirso's Toledan years.

The title of *No le arriendo la ganancia* was a common saying that may be rendered as "Much good may it do him!" or "I wouldn't be in his shoes!"[3] In Tirso's *auto* it refers to Honor, who leaves his country home and his half-brother Recollection, marries Fickleness, and goes to court where he becomes the *privado* of Power. He is an important personage there since the whole life of the court revolves round honor; but when Recollection and his bride Quiet go in search of him they find existence at court impossible, and realize that he is not to be envied. Before long his wife Fickleness has transferred her affections to Power; this drives Honor mad, and his life is in danger. He only recovers health by returning to his village, where the wedding feast of Quiet and Recollection is in progress; Eternal Wisdom is the host, who welcomes His guests to the sacramental meal of the altar.

The lessons of this *auto* are therefore not doctrinal but social and moral. Like several of Calderón's masterpieces in the genre it is concerned with the choice between right and wrong values. Praise of peaceful country life, the trials of *privanza*, the fragility of honor—these are all old themes, but they are well blended together into a dramatic unity. The half-brothers act as foils to each other, and the two ways of life are visually contrasted when, in an excellent stage scene, Power and his lordly retinue pass through the village while out hunting and entice Honor away with them. The vignettes of life at court, where Ignorance is the doctor, Interest the magistrate, and Flattery the clown; the threat to Honor's existence when his wife is unfaithful; and the role of Recollection in restoring him to his senses, all show the allegory to be ingenious and well sustained.

Critics on the whole have been lukewarm about Tirso's *autos*; Vossler,[4] Wardropper,[5] and Nougué[6] all suggest that his talent was for the actualities of the stage and that he lacked the necessary power of abstract thought. But I wonder whether this is not to misunderstand the nature of the genre. Not only is all allegory a transmutation of the abstract into the concrete, but the essence of a sacrament also is that it gives outward and visible form to underlying truths. The *auto sacramental* is therefore doubly committed to a process of exteriorization. The conceptual content of Tirso's *autos* is perfectly clear, and in no way defective; his lessons coincide with those of *auto* after *auto* by Calderón. If he teaches them by means of realistic stage action, recognizable settings, distinctive characters, and lively dialogue full of clever double meanings, he has surely done his job well, rather than the reverse.

II *Prose Collections*

A number of references have already been made to Tirso's two prose miscellanies, *The Country Houses of Toledo* (completed 1621, published 1624) and *Pleasure with Profit* (completed 1632, published 1635). The former figures frequently in studies of Tirso and his works on account of the biographical references and the statements of dramatic theory that it contains. Both works are given detailed examination in André Nougué's *L'œuvre en prose de Tirso de Molina*.

Although both consist largely of prose fiction each also includes dramatic pieces and a quantity of verse. These various elements are enclosed within a fictional framework after the manner of Boccaccio's *Decameron*. *The Country Houses* is one of the first Spanish examples of the framed collection of stories which was to enjoy a great vogue from the 1620s; and its construction is more ingenious than most. A group of lords and ladies escape from the heat of Toledo in the dog days and entertain each other in their country houses with plays, stories, and other diversions. There is the regatta on the Tagus in which Tirso himself took part and won a prize (see above, p. 18); there is a kind of treasure hunt, in which the gallants follow various trails leading to the Castle of the Pursuit of Love where their ladies await them; a racy story is told about a competition between three wives to see who can play the cleverest *burla* on her husband. But at the same time the lords and ladies have themselves been involved in complicated adventures, and these too are narrated in flashback. Before the series of entertainments begins, a very long introduction tells the checkered love story of two of the company whose marriage is now being celebrated; and later the host for the third day regales his guests with the tale of his own recent adventures. This narrative is in turn interrupted and held in suspense while other couples are brought to the fore. In a structure of great intricacy the affairs of three or more pairs of lovers may at any one point be awaiting resolution, and the reader sees the various fictions in a series of receding planes.

The plan of *Pleasure with Profit* is much closer to the simple Boccaccian pattern; and this work with its Horatian title, coming after the Act of Contrition of 1630, bears witness to its author's new seriousness of purpose. The noble company are this time in Madrid and meet to spend the three days of Shrovetide Carnival together, not in the usual merrymaking but in an improving manner more suited to the approach of Lent. In the afternoons instead of comedies they watch *autos sacramentales;* in the mornings they hear stories of the lives of saints. The first of these, *La patrona de las musas* (*The Patron of the Muses*), tells of St. Tecla's rejection of earthly love, her adherence to St. Paul, and her martyrdom; *Los triunfos de la verdad* (*The Triumphs of Truth*) is about St. Clement; and *El bandolero* (*The Bandit*) is the story of an early Mercedarian saint from Catalonia, Pedro Armengol. Verse is also recited, much of it being Tirso's own contributions to various poetic contests in which he had taken part.

Both collections thus incorporate work already in existence: verses, *autos*, plays, and, among the stories, at least the greater part of *The Bandit* which has been shown to date from the early 1620s.[7] Yet in each case it seems that the framework was more than a mere pretext, and sufficient details are given to suggest that the gatherings and performances did actually take place. Nougué has been able to discover real identities for some of the characters of *The Country Houses* and senses a firm stratum of truth beneath its fictions, which contemporary readers may well have been able to interpret as *romans à clef*.[8] But the facts are all heavily gilded. Settings in both works are described not in realistic detail but in terms of baroque conceit and fantasy; and there is everywhere an exaltation of the refined and aristocratic that at times seems almost fawning.

Apart from the rollicking tale of the three tricked husbands and the adventures of the *gracioso*-like servant in the early part of the narrative of the third day, the stories of *The Country Houses* belong to the romantic world of the courtly novel. They derive from both the Italian novella and the much longer Greek or Byzantine novel of adventure, which enjoyed a vogue in the sixteenth and seventeenth centuries and led to such large-scale romances as Lope's *Peregrino en su patria* (*The Pilgrim in his Own Country*) and Cervantes' *Persiles and Sigismunda*. Their staple is the temporary frustration of lovers, often for no very good reason, leading to separation and disguise, long journeys and strange encounters, storms, shipwrecks, and innumerable vicissitudes before ultimate reunion is achieved. The same elements recur in the saintly stories of *Pleasure with Profit*. The action of the liveliest of them, *The Bandit*, includes disguise, elopement, abduction, imprisonment, shipwreck, war, banditry, suicide, and murder, as well as an attempt at martyrdom by hanging; this fails because the saint's body is supported by the Virgin Mary, with whom he enjoys a mystical communion while on the gallows.

The miraculous element is naturally strong in all the religious tales. So too is a show of culture and learning, seen in sententious comments and quotations from the classics, as well as in the theological disputations of *The Triumphs of Truth*, and the court of love scene in *The Bandit*, where the company discuss some of the "cases" previously propounded in Boccaccio's *Filocolo*. Frequent allusions to the rational, sensitive, or irascible appetite, to the vegetative faculties or the three powers of the soul, reveal a heavy reliance on scholastic psychology; while the problem of teaching spiritual lessons through the medium of a literary tradition based on sexual love is solved by a recourse to Platonism.[9]

Although the descriptive prose of *The Country Houses* is often inflated, the narrative style sometimes acquires a certain verve from the momentum of the story, or is enlivened by an apt image; as when a gallant anxious not to wake a sleeping lady treads "as if he had the gout" (I, 32). The language of *Pleasure with Profit*, on the other hand, is nearly all affected and contrived, sometimes to the point of obscuring the meaning. There is a constant sense of striving for effect; statements are embroidered with conceits, actions justified by aphorisms, imagery weighed down with erudition. The verse, too, of the later collection is characterized chiefly by ingenuity. Tirso's competition pieces show his technical mastery of both octosyllabic and Italianate verse forms, and of a variety of modes from the *culto* to the burlesque; but none of them are memorable poetry.

Both works touch on the controversy aroused by the writings of Góngora, and Tirso differentiates between the genuinely *culto* poet and the type he calls the *crítico*, who makes himself ridiculous by his classicizing and distortion of the language. Don Melchor of the country-house company likens the former to a gardener carefully selecting his choicest and most exquisite blooms to make a bouquet, and the latter to a host who serves up a bird with its feathers on, so that his guests have to work hard before they can enjoy it (I, 189). In a long section of *The Bandit* devoted to literary matters the *críticos* are compared to the giant figures carried in Corpus Christi processions, outwardly impressive but stuffed with straw; and the heroine's diction is praised for its freedom from pompous periphrases, undigested metaphors, and words plundered from other tongues.[10]

But if the heroine avoids these blemishes her chronicler unfortunately does not, and much of the prose of *Pleasure with Profit* would seem to exemplify just that kind of pseudoerudite affectation that Tirso seems anxious to condemn. He clearly intended his two prose collections to stamp him as a polished and sophisticated writer who could appeal to a cultivated readership as well as to the common man in the theater; but he can only be judged partially successful. Both works seem curious hybrids, born of material which is largely medieval in origin mismatched with the latest artifices, and sometimes excesses, of baroque style.

III History of the Mercedarian Order

The circumstances of the writing of Tirso's great history of his order were outlined in Chapter I. It was his last major enterprise, and it resulted in a work quite different in subject and scale from anything he had produced before. The rejection of this monumental study, which represented most of the labors of his fifties, must have been one of his saddest disappointments; and the fact that it has remained largely unknown has left the picture of his total achievement very incomplete.

The Mercedarian order has made handsome if belated amends to its illustrious son by the recent publication of this *History* in the two large volumes of Father Manuel Penedo's splendid edition. This work of scholarship which has involved years of research, the transcribing of nearly nine hundred manuscript folios, and the writing of a three-hundred page introduction which is a book in itself, represents a labor no less remarkable than Tirso's own.

In the second part of his introduction, and particularly in Chapters VI, VII, and VIII, Penedo assesses Tirso as a historiographer. He quotes Tirso's own description of his methods—"I rummaged among papers ancient and modern, I read authors and chronicles both printed and in manuscript, I sought information in depositories and archives" (I, cclxiv)—and praises the triumph of synthesis which enabled him to organize this material and build up a coherent account from such a multiplicity of sources. He points to the sound historical criteria that guided the selection, the shrewd personal judgments and evaluations, the avoidance of moral disquisitions, and the strong sense of realism, particularly in the latter part.

The student of literature will turn to Téllez's *History* primarily as a further example of his prose writing. A fairly early chapter (I, 253–59) deals with the same San Pedro Armengol whose story was fictionalized in *The Bandit*, and it is interesting to compare the two versions. The *History*, adhering closely to its sources, discards all such novelistic features as horoscope, undisclosed identity, love intrigues, sea voyages, and adventures, and reduces the phases of Pedro's life to three: a comfortable youth, a period of rebellion and banditry, and repentance in the monastic life. As a Mercedarian he took part in expeditions to ransom captives, and once remained behind as a hostage; it was then that the attempt to hang him and the mystical colloquy with the Virgin took place.

The Pedro Armengol of the *History* is therefore chiefly interesting as one of those figures who switch from depravity to equal extremes of holiness. Tirso comments: "It is remarkable to observe the spiritual advancement over the rest, of those saints who, having first been sinners, undergo a total conversion" (I, 256). It seems very likely that his story as told in *The Bandit* had begun as pure fiction about imaginary characters, and that Tirso grafted the identity and career of the Mercedarian saint on to it in order to make it suitable for inclusion in his religious collection.[11] The language of the later version is more restrained than that of the earlier, though still polished and somewhat mannered. The narrative moves smoothly and not too slowly, and shows its affinity with the technique of the novel by including some passages in direct speech.

As Tirso comes to the events of his own day a more personal note is heard. He criticizes the generalship of the scholarly Zumel by comparing him to a doctor expert in theory who prescribes remedies without regard to the individual patient: "I, at least, would prefer a moderately learned doctor who had experience and took temperaments into account, to a professor who taught generalities in his faculty and seldom felt pulses." Some recent provincials, too, have been "eagle-eyed in speculation but blind as moles in practical matters" (II, 264).

When he has actually been present at the events he records he is sometimes able to enliven his accounts with sense impressions. Such is the case with the especially joyful *Te Deum* sung in the cloisters at Guadalajara after the elections at the 1618 chapter (II, 402); or the spontaneous demonstrations in Santo Domingo in honor of the Immaculate Conception, when sailors leapt from their boats challengingly brandishing weapons and torches, and small boys marched through the streets carrying paper banners and candles bought with money they had wheedled from their mothers (II, 357).

It would be a mistake, however, to think that Tirso has either the descriptive or the narrative powers of a Cervantes. Even when he has been an eyewitness his accounts are less vivid than those of many an imagined scene by the master of Spanish prose. Much of the *History* is quite readable, but little of it is memorable. Where its style is not mannered or contrived it tends to be wordy, with an unsyntactical piling of clause upon clause which suggests that its author was writing at great speed. The chronicle of his order would not by itself have won him literary fame. But it is a major historical achievement, and of no small interest for the light it sheds on Gabriel Téllez the man and the writer in the years after his work for the theater was done.

CHAPTER 11

Conclusion

I Gabriel Téllez the Man

TO most modern readers there is something puzzling about the figure of Gabriel Téllez, a monk respected and honored in his religious order, yet in touch with the public theaters and the author of many frivolous and by no means always exemplary works of entertainment. It was this apparent dichotomy that led some of his early critics to assume, wrongly as it turned out, that he had a long experience of the world before entering the cloister. To his contemporaries, used as they were to Lope de Vega's disregard of his priestly orders and to the prolonged absenteeism of such ecclesiastical functionaries as Góngora and Mira de Amescua, the anomaly may not have seemed so great; though the terms of Tirso's condemnation in 1625, whatever its ultimate cause, show that some impropriety was felt to exist.

A study of his writings reveals a similar incompatibility between high and sincerely held ideals, and baser emotions from which he was never able to break free. On the one hand there are the exaltations of friendship and loyalty, and the subordination of the code of honor to ideals of prudence and forgiveness, remarkable in the Golden Age theater which extracts so much drama from the avenging of honor. On the other hand, *The Country Houses* of 1624 and the 1625 insertions in *Antona García* contain bitter allusions to envious competitors, and this note of hostility is still being struck a decade later in the prologues to the later *partes*. Moreover his early friendly relations with Lope were clearly disrupted in the 1620s, and his name is conspicuously absent from the list of those poets who contributed to a posthumous eulogy of Lope after his death in 1635. It seems likely that after the promise of his Toledan years Tirso foresaw a glorious future for himself on his return to Madrid; and the opposition that he then met set up in him a rancor that neither his own preaching of forgiveness nor his increased devotion and Act of Contrition in 1630 was able totally to dispel.

This impression of a deeply sensitive man whose wounds did not heal is borne out by the strange episode of an anonymous verse which linked his name with that of his fellow dramatist Alarcón. The verse was apparently daubed on the whitewashed wall of a confectioner's shop where playbills were normally posted, and it read:

> ¡Vítor don Juan de Alarcón
> y el fraile de la Merced!
> —por ensuciar la pared,
> y no por otra razón.

This could be taken to mean "Hurrah for Don Juan de Alarcón and the Mercedarian friar!—I say this only for the sake of dirtying the wall, and for no other reason"; in other words, they had no claim to fame as playwrights. But the third line could also mean "for having dirtied the wall," implying some indecency on the part of the two dramatists; and that Tirso took it in some such way is apparent from the half-dozen smarting allusions to the verse found in his plays, most of them probably inserted when the works were being prepared for print. In 1635 the Conde de la Roca urged Tirso to forget the libel and to go on writing, thus showing that the insult had continued to rankle.

Professor Kennedy treats the episode fully in Chapter VII of *Studies in Tirso, I*. Among other evidence, Roca's linking of the scurrilous verse with Tirso's ceasing to write leads her to connect it with the dramatist's opposition to Olivares and his palace clique of Andalusian poets, and to suggest that its authors were probably Hurtado de Mendoza and Vélez de Guevara. Certainly some such connection with the great antagonism of his life would seem necessary to account for his lasting resentment of what would otherwise seem pretty innocuous, if distasteful, graffiti.[1]

A tendency toward personal involvement in controversy may perhaps have been fostered by the conditions of celibate life. In the case of a monk who wrote hundreds of plays with a strong love interest, it is pertinent to enquire what his relations with women were. Despite his contacts with worldly society and with the theater there is no record of any sexual scandal in his life; nor are his depictions of women and of love, any more than those of most

Golden Age dramatists, so realistically convincing as to suggest that they were based on personal experience.

There are a few passages relating to love in his writings that it is tempting to read as autobiographical allusions. The self-sacrifice of the melancholic Rogerio (I, 114a), and Leonisa's resolve to love platonically when it seems that she cannot marry (104a), have an unusually sincere ring about them; and the impression of a personal statement on the author's part is intensified when very similar language is seen to be used by the lovers of *The Bandit,* Laurisana and Pedro Armengol (fols. 223, 239)—particularly as the latter goes on to become a Mercedarian monk. Blanca de los Ríos has pointed to the sonnet which opens Act II of *El castigo del penséque* (*The Penalty for 'Thinking That'*), and which contains the striking quatrain: "He who promises never to love for the rest of his life, and curbs his will in the face of temptation, let him dry up the waters of the sea or count its sands, still the winds or measure the infinite" (I, 555b); and she suggests that here too may be glimpsed some personal drama of renunciation on Tirso's part. On the other hand, when Lisena of *Jealous but Prudent* hesitates to confide her amorous secrets to one who has herself never loved, Diana's reply could well be read as Tirso's statement of his own position: "I know the blind passion of love perhaps better than those who draw its wages and reach the center of its sphere; for the onlooker has a better grasp of the game than the player" (I, 1107a); and the *gracioso* of the *Achilles,* who is almost certainly stepping out of his role to become Tirso's mouthpiece in his catalog of the arms he bears, has moments before described himself as a eunuch (I, 1839b). Yet in the last resort all these characters are speaking for themselves, and any autobiographical interpretation of their words can only be conjectural.

The total impression of Gabriel Téllez that emerges from his writings is of a man who probably lacked any advantages of birth but was aware of his literary talent and sharp mind, and no doubt saw the life of a religious community as the best road to intellectual advancement. He seems not to have been irked by its celibacy, to have worked hard in it and won its respect, and to have held high political and moral ideals. At the same time he was no saint, and when he found his progress blocked—more probably because of his own outspokenness and the jealousy of others than for the reasons of birth proposed by Blanca de los Ríos—his pride and ambition turned into a resentment which he never shook off, and which, issuing in further polemic writings, was almost certainly the ultimate cause of his second silencing and exile.

II *Tirso de Molina the Dramatist*

The writer Montalbán, approving Tirso's Fourth *parte* for publication in 1635, praises his theater for its aphorisms and conceits, its satire, humor and wit, the intricacy of its plots, its satisfying cadences, and the wisdom of its moral teaching.[2] His approbation gives some idea of the literary qualities prized in Tirso's own day. The nineteenth-century critics who prefaced the Hartzenbusch collection of 1848[3] had largely lost sight of the moral dramas, and criticized the unmaidenly conduct of the comedy heroines and the repetitive nature of the plots; but they were unanimous in their praise of dialogue, wit, and lively comic scenes.

On the question of the plots Tirso himself would have sided with Montalbán. He was proud of his fecundity in inventing *trazas*, and scorned dramatists who reworked the plots of others. Yet it must be admitted that the complexity of his intrigues sometimes runs ahead of any logical motivation, as for example in *Love Turned Doctor;* and that to read his comedies one after the other is to realize how very often he relies on the same old devices. His best-known formula is the heroine pursuing and angling for her man, who assumes first a masculine and then a second feminine identity; she figures in *Don Gil of the Green Breeches, The Village Girl of La Sagra, Love Turned Doctor,* and elsewhere. Other devices recur in other comedies: *The Shy Man at Court, Through Basement and Hatch,* and *Pious Martha* all present pairs of sisters and the stratagems of one of the girls to avoid an arranged match and marry for love; in the two latter plays the unwelcome suitor is a rich old man returned from the Indies; in the two former, the suitor never arrives on the scene but constitutes a gradually approaching threat. Scenes of madness are to be found in plays as different as *The Village Girl of La Sagra, True Friendship,* and the *Achilles*. The world of Tirso's comedies offers a series of endless variations on a limited number of themes. Each play by itself makes excellent entertainment, but all are drawn out of the same not very capacious bag of tricks.

Tirso's fairly frequent choice of proverbs, or parts of proverbs, as titles for his comedies illustrates his largely cerebral approach, his tendency to start from a concept or idea rather than from a human situation. It has already been seen how in the case of *The Shy Man at Court* the credibility of Mireno's character is sacrificed to the requirements of the title. Occasionally the proverb will be used with moral or sententious intent, but it is more often simply a peg on which to hang a formula plot.[4]

As a humorist Tirso can scarcely be faulted. The obscenities of his *graciosos* become a little tedious, and his social satire on foibles of dress and behavior is fairly conventional. Yet he is a master of comic characters like Marta; of comic situations such as Magdalena trying to get the shy Mireno to woo her, or the romantic Melchor's collapse in the filthy street; and above all, as his critics in all ages have seen, of superbly comic dialogue. The agile verbal sparring of man and maidservant in *Jealous but Prudent* (I, 1113–15), and Ventura's torrents of wit throughout *Jealous of Herself*, show how Tirso can play and juggle with words. He had a keen ear for language, as well as a facility in writing, and he makes full use of it for comic effect.

There is evidence of a more intellectual and literary humor, too, in the satirical digs at Góngora and the *tramoyistas*, and the gentle mockery of Lope's *Arcadia*; while a clever sonnet on a toothpick in *Feigned Arcady* (II, 1419–20) shows a range of witty conceits almost worthy of Quevedo.[5]

Critical consideration of Tirso's language has for the most part concerned itself with the dialogue and wit, but the variety of his styles should not be overlooked. As well as satirizing Góngora he can also imitate him, with by no means unpleasing results; the *culto* passages in which Rogerio describes his first sight of Leonisa (I, 88), and Don Juan of *The Reluctant Favorite* his glimpse of the Infanta taking her bathe (III, 1077–78), are excellent examples. Neither is he a mean rhetorician. Just as wickedness is a more dramatic quality than goodness, so anger, spite, and indignation are the moods that lend themselves to most forceful expression, and these Tirso can convey in powerful speeches using all the arts of oratory; witness Achilles, in the person of Nereida, defending his own behavior (I, 1828–29); Margarita of *Who Never Falls* (III, 847–48) and Liberio of *Enough is as Good as a Feast* (I, 986) inveighing against their respective fathers; even Inés rounding on "Don Gil" when she thinks "he" has been untrue (I, 1639–40). Tirso can use the heavy guns as well as the glancing rapier.

It is not only when employing rhetoric or the *culto* manner that he shows his skill in imagery. He is always ready with the apt analogy, on whatever level, as a few examples from *The Shy Man at*

Court will show: a woman who knows a secret is in travail until she can bring it forth (I, 305b); the voluminous slashed breeches Tarso borrows are as complicated as an astrolabe (313b); Antonio has flown into the trap of love like a bird alighting on a limed branch (325a); undeclared love is like a rolled-up Flemish painting (344b). At a later stage he uses imagery more subtly too, repeating and dwelling on a simile or metaphor in such a way as to emphasize his theme; such is the case with the conceit of love as appetite for food, sustained through much of *Tamar's Vengeance,* and with the recurrent metaphors of serpents and fire, darkness and cold in *The Trickster of Seville.*[6]

Some critics have praised Tirso's lyricism, referring to the many delightful rustic songs included in his plays. One such lyric repeatedly quoted is the milling song, "Al molino del amor/ alegre la la niña va" ("The girl goes joyfully to the mill of love"), sung in *Don Gil of the Green Breeches* (I, 1615). Tirso certainly made much use of popular material in lyric interludes, as did both Lope and Shakespeare, and with none of the three is it easy to know when these songs are their own compositions, and when they are incorporating traditional and popular verses already familiar to their audiences. It must be assumed that many of Tirso's songs are his own work, although in imitation of the popular manner, and if this is so it is a genre in which he may be judged very successful.[7]

It is difficult to say the same for the other pieces of a lyric nature, such as sonnets and odes, that can be extracted from his plays, or to see a high poetic quality in his drama as a whole. In the extensive rereading of his theater that I have undertaken for the purpose of writing this book, I have been struck by many fine images and forceful expressions, but I have only once found myself arrested by what seemed to me genuine poetry. This was in the opening words of *Pious Martha.* Marta, foreseeing no possibility of a happy ending to the pangs of love, contrasts her sufferings with those of the ploughing ox, who can at least hope for respite in the evening:

> El tardo buey, atado a la coyunda,
> la noche espera, y la cerviz levanta. (II, 354a)
> (The sluggish ox, roped to the heavy yoke,
> Looks forward to the night, and lifts his head.)

Not merely the apt image, but also the smooth hendecasyllabic rhythm, the slow pace and thick, dull sounds suggestive of the beast's movement, and the perfect economy of expression, make these lines poetically memorable; but the remaining lines of the sonnet, and the one that follows it, are unrhythmical, repetitive, and wordy. It might be possible to find a few other passages of real poetry, but not many. An easy versifier, a clever practitioner of a variety of styles, a master of dramatic dialogue, Tirso is all these; but hardly a great lyric poet.

Are the qualities so far considered, and those listed by Montalbán, enough to justify Tirso's being considered a "world author"? The modern reader probably looks for something more: some depth of human understanding, some revelation of meaning and truth, not through explicit preaching nor even through an action deliberately chosen to exemplify a moral lesson, but through an artistic representation of the wonder and horror, the joy and pain, the comedy and tragedy of life as it really is. He will not find it consistently, or even often, in Tirso. Tirso is primarily an entertainer and secondly a preacher, and does not often explore the depths.

Nevertheless I think it is possible to distinguish between the two periods of his dramatic production, and to see how the skill and virtuosity of his Toledan years matured on his return to Madrid. Partly because he was older, more traveled, and more experienced, partly no doubt because of the very frustrations that he resented so deeply, his artistry was now more refined and his penetration sharper. This enabled him, among much that is still admittedly second-rate, to invest conventional intrigues with deeper significance, turning the cloister-house of *Through Basement and Hatch* into a sexual symbol and the reluctant *privado* Don Juan into the voice of conscience. It permitted him to improve on his own earlier work, dignifying the shallow story of *That's Business!* with a noble character-study of an intellectual, and, if the general assumptions about authorship and dating are correct, giving to *What Long Credit*, or its original, the greater artistic coherence of *The Trickster of Seville*. And it resulted in those masterly dramatizations of Bible stories that are in my opinion among the greatest of his works.

In *Tamar's Vengeance* and *The Wife who Rules the Roost*, Tirso does not flinch from the horrible and brutal, but uses it to lead his audience into deeper understanding. Amnon is guilty, but partly because of his father's guilt before him; and when he in turn becomes a victim we are led to question Tamar's own principles which have demanded vengeance, and to share in David's realization of the bewildering inextricability of right and wrong. Naboth dies a gruesome death, but the stones that kill him are invested with rich symbolism, itself symbolic of the way in which horror and evil can be alchemized by the tragedian into great aesthetic beauty.

Tirso is, as all but the most partisan of his critics have had to admit, a remarkably uneven dramatist. He can reach impressive heights, and he can sink very low. There is scarcely any play of his that is not somehow flawed. The comparison with his two great Spanish contemporaries is inevitable, and it reveals him as lacking the technical excellence, the harmony, and the humanity of Lope, and the majesty and intellectual rigor of Calderón. But he has his own gifts, gifts of vivacity and wit, of skill in simile and symbol, of a high moral sense linked to a sturdy independence of mind; his best plays have all the power of great art; and it is a major contribution to the world's drama that we owe to this versatile Mercedarian monk.

Notes and References

Chapter One

1. Miguel L. Ríos, "Tirso de Molina no es bastardo," and Manuel Penedo, "Ampliación al trabajo del P. Ríos 'Tirso no es bastardo,' " both in *Tirso de Molina* (Madrid: Revista Estudios, 1949), pp. 1–13 and 14–18.
2. Mario Penna, *Don Giovanni e il mistero di Tirso* (Torino, 1958).
3. José Rus Lucenilla, "Tirso de Molina," *Reconquista*, nos. 3–6 (Guadalajara, March–June 1951).
4. Henry Sullivan, "Was Gaspar Lucas Hidalgo the Godfather of Tirso de Molina?" *Bulletin of the Comediantes* 26 (1974), 5–11.
5. Guillermo Guastavino Gallent, "Notas tirsianas II," *Revista de Archivos, Bibliotecas y Museos* 69 (1961), 817–20.
6. Tirso de Molina, *Historia general de la Orden de Nuestra Señora de las Mercedes*, Introducción y primera edición crítica por Fray Manuel Penedo Rey, 2 vols. (Madrid: Provincia de la Merced de Castilla, Colección Revista Estudios, 1973, 1974). On the date of Tirso's birth see I, xxiii–xxxv.
7. Penedo argues vigorously for a date of birth in the first three weeks of 1581. Anything earlier, he thinks, would not square with the 1616 authorization; and Tirso's admission to the Mercedarian order on 20 January 1600 probably took place when he was nineteen. As regards the first of these arguments, however, even January 1581 would not square with the authorization as it stands, and if this document cannot be taken literally it cannot prove anything. As regards the second, Penedo seems to assume that Tirso joined the order on or immediately after his birthday, but offers no evidence for this. Unless this was the case the evidence Penedo puts forward for January 1581 would be equally valid for any date during the preceding eleven months.
8. Tirso de Molina, *Los cigarrales de Toledo*, 2 vols. (Madrid: Espasa-Calpe, 1942), I, 117. Future references to this work will be to this edition.
9. Ruth Lee Kennedy, *Studies in Tirso, I: The Dramatist and his Competitors, 1620-26*, North Carolina Studies in the Romance Languages and Literatures (Chapel Hill, 1974), pp. 68–69.
10. Tirso de Molina, *Obras dramáticas completas*, edición crítica por

Blanca de los Ríos, 3 vols. (Madrid: Aguilar, 1946, 1952, and 1958), I, lxxxviii. All future references to Blanca de los Ríos, and to Tirso's plays, will be to this edition.

11. André Nougué, *L'œuvre en prose de Tirso de Molina* (Toulouse, 1962), pp. 159-71.

12. See the following articles by Gerald E. Wade: "*El burlador de Sevilla:* the Tenorios and the Ulloas," *Symposium* 19 (1965), 249-58; "Tirso's *Cigarrales de Toledo:* Some Clarifications and Identifications," *Hispanic Review* 33 (1965), 246-72; "Tirso's Friends," *Bulletin of the Comediantes* 19 (1967), 1-6; "Character Names in Some of Tirso's Comedies," *Hispanic Review* 36 (1968), 1-34; "Tirso and the Court Circle," in *Homage to John M. Hill*, ed. Walter Poesse (Bloomington: Indiana University Press, 1968), pp. 243-58; and "*La celosa de sí misma* de Tirso de Molina," in *Homenaje al Profesor William L. Fichter*, ed. A. David Kossoff and José Amor y Vázquez (Madrid: Castalia, 1971), pp. 755-63.

13. *Studies in Tirso, I*, pp. 70, 71.

14. Wade, *Hispanic Review* 36 (1968), p. 31.

15. Gerald E. Wade, "Tirso's Earliest Use of his Pseudonym," *Hispania* 47 (1964), 757-59.

16. Angela B. Dellepiane, in *Presencia de América en la obra de Tirso de Molina* (Madrid: Revista Estudios, 1968), records many mentions of Latin American elements in Tirso's theater, but they are mostly incidental, and few reflect any personal experience.

17. See J. H. Elliott, *Imperial Spain 1469-1716* (Harmondsworth: Penguin, 1963), pp. 323-49.

18. Tirso de Molina, *Antona García*, ed. Margaret Wilson (Manchester: Manchester University Press, 1957). See introduction, pp. xxii-xxv.

19. *Studies in Tirso, I*, Chapter II.

20. Published by M. Menéndez Pelayo in *Revista de Archivos, Bibliotecas y Museos* 18 (1908), 1-17, 243-56; 19 (1908), 262-73; and 21 (1909), 139-57 and 567-70.

Chapter Two

1. See Ruth L. Kennedy, *Studies in Tirso, I*, 169-73.

2. Jaime Moll, "Diez años sin licencias para imprimir comedias y novelas en los reinos de Castilla, 1625-1634," *Boletín de la Real Academia Española* 54 (1974), 97-103.

3. Jaime Moll, "El problema bibliográfico de la 'Primera parte de Comedias' de Tirso de Molina," in *Homenaje a Guillermo Guastavino* (Madrid, 1974), pp. 85-94.

4. For the preliminaries and bibliographical details of all Tirso's *partes*, see E. Cotarelo's "Discurso preliminar" in his edition of *Comedias de Tirso de Molina*, vol. I, in *Nueva Biblioteca de Autores Españoles*, vol. 4 (Madrid, 1906).

5. Introduction to *History of the Mercedarian Order*, I, ci.
6. See her statement on *Siempre ayuda la verdad* in *Studies in Tirso*, I, p. 340.
7. Professor Kennedy was the first to suggest, contrary to the general assumption, that *Esto sí que es negociar* was the earlier of these two plays (see *Hispanic Review* 11 [1943], p. 26). I believe that she is right, and I have studied the relationship between the two more closely in an article to be published in the homage volume which Professor Vern G. Williamsen is preparing in her honor.
8. *Comedias de Tirso de Molina*, I, lxi.
9. Ruth Lee Kennedy, "Tirso's *Cautela contra cautela:* its Authenticity in his Theatre and its Importance," *Revista de Archivos, Bibliotecas y Museos* 75 (1968–1972), 325–53.
10. Ruth Lee Kennedy, "Quiteria, comedianta toledana," *Revista Hispánica Moderna* 37 (1972–1973), 10.
11. Blanca de los Ríos (I, cxii) reproduces the relevant document, in which the titles of the last two plays are given as *Sixto Quinto* and *Saber guardar su hacienda*. *Sixto Quinto* is clearly *La elección por la virtud*. *Saber guardar su hacienda* was long thought to be lost, but José López Navío has shown that this was almost certainly the play later known as *Tanto es lo de más como lo de menos;* see "Una comedia de Tirso que no está perdida," *Estudios* 16 (1960), 331–47.
12. See Blanca de los Ríos, I, cxvi–cxvii and cxxiv, and Gerald E. Wade, "Tirso's *Santa Juana*, Primera parte," *Modern Language Notes* 49 (1934), 13–18.
13. F. de B. San Román, *Lope de Vega, los cómicos toledanos y el poeta sastre* (Madrid, 1935), pp. lxxviii–lxxix.
14. *Todo es dar en una cosa, Amazonas en las Indias, La lealtad contra la envidia.*
15. Ruth Lee Kennedy, "Tirso's *Desde Toledo a Madrid:* its Date and Place of Composition," in *Homenaje a William L. Fichter*, pp. 357–66.
16. See especially "Certain Phases of the Sumptuary Decrees of 1623 and their Relation to Tirso's Theatre," *Hispanic Review* 10 (1942), 91–115; "On the Date of Five Plays by Tirso de Molina," *Hispanic Review* 10 (1942), 183–214; and "Studies for the Chronology of Tirso's Theatre," *Hispanic Review* 11 (1943), 17–46. There is further information on dating to be found throughout Professor Kennedy's writings on Tirso.
17. S. Griswold Morley and Courtney Bruerton, *The Chronology of Lope de Vega's* Comedias (New York: Modern Language Association of America, 1940; revised Spanish edition, Madrid: Gredos, 1968).
18. Courtney Bruerton, reviews of Volumes I and II of Tirso's *Obras dramáticas completas*, ed. Blanca de los Ríos, in *Nueva Revista de Filología Hispánica* 3 (1949), 189–96, and 8 (1954), 200–203. A much earlier study of this type was that by S. G. Morley, "The Use of Verse Forms in Tirso de

Molina," *Bulletin Hispanique* 7 (1905), 387–408; but though Morley makes interesting comments on Tirso's use of certain meters he was not able to conclude anything about the chronology of his theater.

19. André Nougué, "*La venganza de Tamar* de Tirso de Molina. Notes pour l'établissement du texte. Problème de la datation," *Bulletin Hispanique* 73 (1971), 104–24.

20. In addition to the articles already referred to, see Gerald E. Wade, "El escenario histórico y la fecha de *Amar por razón de estado*, in *Tirso de Molina* (Madrid: Revista Estudios, 1949), pp. 657–70; "Tirso's *Privar contra su gusto*," *Kentucky Romance Quarterly* 17 (1970), 93–107; and G. E. Wade and Jaime José González, "Tirso de Molina and the Gonzagas," *Hispania* 55 (1972), 264–77.

Chapter Three

1. See O. Arróniz, *La influencia italiana en el nacimiento de la comedia española* (Madrid: Gredos, 1969).

2. See R. Froldi, *Lope de Vega y la formación de la comedia* (Salamanca: Anaya, 1968); John G. Weiger, *The Valencian Dramatists of Spain's Golden Age* (Boston: Twayne, 1976).

3. Tirso de Molina, *El vergonzoso en palacio*, ed. Francisco Ayala (Madrid: Castalia, 1971).

4. Letter of 25–26 July 1615, in *Epistolario de Lope de Vega*, ed. A. González de Amezúa y Mayo, 4 vols. (Madrid, 1935–1943), III, 206.

5. See Gerald E. Wade, "La comicidad de *Don Gil de las calzas verdes* de Tirso de Molina," *Revista de Archivos, Bibliotecas y Museos* 76 (1973), 475–86.

6. On the erotic significance of hands in Golden Age drama see Margaret Wilson, "*Comedia* Lovers and the Proprieties," *Bulletin of the Comediantes* 24 (1972), 31–36.

7. This paragraph is indebted to a paper on *La celosa* given by Dr. P. Halkhoree to a conference of British Hispanists at Southampton in 1971, and to the subsequent discussion. Dr. Halkhoree is preparing an edition of the play.

8. "Literary and Political Satire in Tirso's *La fingida Arcadia*," first published in *The Renaissance Reconsidered*, Smith College Studies in History, 44 (Northampton, Mass., 1964), and reprinted with slight revisions in *Studies in Tirso, I*.

9. For a detailed study of the relations between Lope and Tirso during this period see *Studies in Tirso, I*, Chapter III.

10. See N. D. Shergold, *A History of the Spanish Stage* (Oxford: Oxford University Press, 1967), pp. 229–30.

Chapter Four

1. Noël Salomon, *Recherches sur le thème paysan dans la 'comedia' au temps de Lope de Vega* (Bordeaux, 1965).

2. R. O. Jones, "Poets and Peasants," in *Homenaje a William L. Fichter*, pp. 341–55.
3. See Penedo, *History*, I, xcii–xciii.
4. *Recherches sur le thème paysan*, 674–78.
5. For a survey of the Galician material in Tirso's theater see Gumersindo Placer, "Tirso y Galicia," in *Tirso de Molina* (Madrid: Revista Estudios, 1949), pp. 415–78.
6. See N. D. Shergold and J. E. Varey, "Some Palace Performances of Seventeenth-century Plays," *Bulletin of Hispanic Studies* 40 (1963), 226.
7. For an excellent evocation of the mood of this period see *Studies in Tirso*, I, Chapter I.
8. P. Halkhoree, "Satire and Symbolism in the Structure of Tirso de Molina's *Por el sótano y el torno*," *Forum for Modern Language Studies* 4 (1968), 374–86.
9. See Serge Maurel, *L'univers dramatique de Tirso de Molina* (Poitiers: Université de Poitiers, 1971), pp. 195–210.

Chapter Five

1. *El amor médico* has been highly praised by many critics, including Alonso Zamora Vicente and María Josefa Canellada de Zamora who edited it for Clásicos Castellanos in 1947. Serge Maurel's excellent analysis in *L'univers dramatique de Tirso de Molina*, pp. 232–38, rectifies the balance.
2. See Ruth Lee Kennedy, "The Dates of *El amor médico* and *Escarmientos para el cuerdo* (Tirso's Supposed Trip to Portugal in 1619)," *Reflexión 2* 1 (1972), 11–33. Professor Kennedy believes that though *El amor médico* may have been written in 1621 and retouched later, it is more likely that it dates entirely from 1625.
3. See the useful analysis by Everett W. Hesse and William C. McCrary, "The Mars-Venus Struggle in Tirso's *El Aquiles*," *Bulletin of Hispanic Studies* 33 (1956), 138–51.
4. The only other instance in Golden Age drama that I can recall is Hercules' dressing as a woman in Calderón's *Fieras afemina amor*; this was a much later play, and not written for the public theaters.
5. Jaime Asensio, "Casos de amor en el teatro de Tirso de Molina," *Cuadernos Hispanoamericanos* 97 (1974), 1–33.
6. See Cyril A. Jones, "Tirso de Molina's *El melancólico* and Cervantes' *El licenciado Vidriera*: a Common Link in Huarte's *Examen de ingenios?*" in *Studia Iberica: Festschrift für Hans Flasche*, ed. K.-H. Körner and K. Rühl (Bern and Munich, 1973), 295–305.

Chapter Six

1. See Margaret Wilson, "Tirso and *pundonor*: a Note on *El celoso prudente*," *Bulletin of Hispanic Studies* 38 (1961), 120–25.
2. Tirso de Molina, *La venganza de Tamar*, ed. A.K.G. Paterson (Cambridge: Cambridge University Press, 1969).

3. Ruth Lee Kennedy, "Notes on Two Interrelated Plays of Tirso, *El amor y el amistad* and *Ventura te dé Dios, hijo*," *Hispanic Review* 28 (1960), 189–214.
4. "Tirso de Molina and the Gonzagas," *Hispania* 55 (1972), 264–77.

Chapter Seven

1. J. H. Elliott, *Imperial Spain 1469–1716*, p. 325.
2. Gerald E. Wade, "Tirso's *Privar contra su gusto*," *Kentucky Romance Quarterly* 17 (1970), 93–107.
3. Ruth Lee Kennedy, "*La prudencia en la mujer* and the Ambient that Brought it Forth," *Publications of the Modern Language Association of America* 63 (1948), 1131–90; also published in Spanish in *Tirso de Molina* (Madrid: Revista Estudios, 1949), pp. 223–93.
4. Ion Tudor Agheana gives a rather different assessment of her character in *The Situational Drama of Tirso de Molina* (New York: Plaza Mayor, 1972), pp. 43–50.
5. Edward M. Wilson and Duncan Moir, *A Literary History of Spain. The Golden Age: Drama 1492–1700* (London: Benn, 1971), p. 96.
6. For the full historical background, and Tirso's adaptation of it, see the introduction to the edition of this play by Margaret Wilson (Manchester: Manchester University Press, 1957).
7. Serge Maurel is not impressed by this aspect of Antona and sees the play simply as "de l'histoire pour rire" (*L'univers dramatique de Tirso de Molina*, pp. 381–84). But is this not to assume that it must necessarily have a consistency of tone, when in fact many of Tirso's plays do not?

Chapter Eight

1. Karl Vossler, *Lecciones sobre Tirso de Molina* (Madrid: Taurus, 1965), p. 51.
2. Their sources are identified by Maurel, Book I, Part I, Chapter 2.
3. P. 351.
4. See p. 33 of the edition by William M. Whitby and Robert R. Anderson of *La fianza satisfecha*, ascribed to Lope de Vega, for the popularity of the verses beginning "Larga cuenta que dar de tiempo largo."
5. Noël Salomon (*Recherches sur le thème paysan*, pp. 864–83) and Serge Maurel (*L'univers dramatique de Tirso de Molina*, pp. 285–310) have both studied closely the relationship between *Fuenteovejuna*, *Santa Juana*, and *La dama del olivar*, and the chronology indicated here is that proposed by them.
6. See Maurel, pp. 133–35.
7. Admittedly the descent of fire from heaven might have presented problems of staging; though Tirso rose to the challenge of the ravens who took food to Elijah in the desert and cleverly tightened the structure of his play by making them snatch the morsels beforehand from the table of Ahab and Jezebel.

8. *Studies in Tirso,* I, p. 180, note 47.
9. J. C. J. Metford, "Tirso de Molina and the Conde-Duque de Olivares," *Bulletin of Hispanic Studies* 36 (1959), 15–27. Another article by Professor Metford, "Tirso de Molina's Old Testament Plays," *Bulletin of Hispanic Studies* 27 (1950), 149–63, is also of interest for this facet of Tirso's theater.
10. Jaime Asensio, "Sobre *Tanto es lo de más como lo de menos* de Tirso de Molina," *Reflexión 2* 2 (1973), 21–37.

Chapter Nine

1. This phrase, which occurs quite often in Golden Age literature, was that chanted by the town crier who preceded criminals on their way to execution.
2. The unity of the work is well argued by Daniel Rogers in "Fearful Symmetry: the Ending of *El burlador de Sevilla*," *Bulletin of Hispanic Studies* 41 (1964), 141–59.
3. See Gerald E. Wade and Robert J. Mayberry, "*Tan largo me lo fiáis* and *El burlador de Sevilla,*" *Bulletin of the Comediantes* 14 (1962), 1–16, and Albert E. Sloman, "The Two Versions of *El burlador de Sevilla,*" *Bulletin of Hispanic Studies* 42 (1965), 18–33.
4. See for instance the sonnet in which Margarita, of *Who Never Falls*, promises to pay off her debt of sin by installments and asks God not to distrain (III, 879a); and Liberio's argument with Lázaro about mortgages, securities, and deposits in heavenly banks (I, 998).
5. See the introduction to *El burlador de Sevilla y convidado de piedra*, ed. Gerald E. Wade (New York: Scribner's, 1969), and also Gerald E. Wade, "The Authorship and the Date of Composition of *El burlador de Sevilla,*" *Hispanófila*, no. 32 (1968), pp. 1–22.
6. See Alan K. G. Paterson, "Tirso de Molina: Two Bibliographical Studies," *Hispanic Review* 35 (1967), 43–68, and the dissenting article by Ruth Lee Kennedy, "Did Tirso Send to Press a *Primera Parte* of Madrid (1626) which Contained *El condenado por desconfiado?*" *Hispanic Review* 41 (1973), 261–74.
7. The play has been studied by Jaime Asensio, "Los desengaños de *El mayor desengaño,*" in *Homenaje a Guillermo Guastavino*, pp. 149–69.
8. Mr. Rogers has reminded me that Nineucio is another Tirsian character who goes to hell; although in his case this is required by the biblical parable. Yet another is Doroteo of the *auto La madrina del cielo*, assuming this work to be by Tirso (see Chapter 10); and we are also told in *Who Never Falls* that Margarita's dead mother is in hell, and for no worse sin than having brought her daughter up too leniently (III, 866b).
9. Professor Kennedy's arguments, based largely on the literary qualities of the work, are set out in an article entitled "Did Tirso Write *El condenado por desconfiado?*" to be published in the *Kentucky Romance Quarterly*. I am very grateful to her for letting me see a copy of this article.

10. See R. Menéndez Pidal, *Estudios literarios* (Buenos Aires: Austral, 1938, containing essays originally published in 1902–1906); E. Cotarelo, "Ultimos estudios acerca de *El burlador de Sevilla*," *Revista de Archivos, Bibliotecas y Museos* 18 (1908), 75–86; and C. V. Aubrun, "Le *Don Juan* de Tirso de Molina: Essai d'interprétation," *Bulletin Hispanique* 59 (1957), 26–61.
11. Tirso de Molina, *Obras dramáticas completas*, II, 425–27.
12. Pp. 517–22.
13. Tirso de Molina, *El condenado por desconfiado*, ed. Daniel Rogers (Oxford: Pergamon, 1974).
14. P. 37.
15. Ruth Lee Kennedy, "*El condenado por desconfiado*: its Ambient and its Date of Composition," in *Homenaje a Guillermo Guastavino*, pp. 213–51.
16. J. Casalduero stresses the clash between the temporal and the eternal in the first chapter of his *Contribución al estudio del tema de Don Juan en el teatro español* (Madrid: Ediciones José Porrúa Turanzas, 1975; first published in Smith College Studies in Modern Languages, 1938).
17. Edition of *La fianza satisfecha*, pp. 43–48.
18. A. A. Parker, "Santos y bandoleros en el teatro español del Siglo de Oro," *Arbor* 13 (1949), 395–416.
19. Edition of *La fianza satisfecha*, pp. 46–47.
20. P. 555.
21. On Paulo as a psychological case see Carlos A. Pérez, "Verosimilitud psicológica de *El condenado por desconfiado*," *Hispanófila*, no. 27 (1966), pp. 1–21.
22. P. 36.
23. The point is well made by Melveena McKendrick in *Woman and Society in the Spanish Drama of the Golden Age: a Study of the "Mujer varonil"* (Cambridge: Cambridge University Press, 1974), pp. 158–59.
24. Bruce W. Wardropper effectively underlines this contrast between the low moral standards of most of the characters and the compassion of Catalinón, who "was aware that the obverse of a *burla* is tragedy"; see "*El burlador de Sevilla*: a Tragedy of Errors," *Philological Quarterly* 36 (1957), 61–71.
25. Although spectacular effects could be achieved in the public theaters by means of *tramoyas* there was little actual scenery, and since performances took place in the afternoon, in roofless theaters, there could be no real darkness; but the audiences, like those of Shakespeare's plays, were evidently able to use their imaginations.
26. *Imperial Spain 1469–1716*, pp. 298–99.

Chapter Ten

1. See the introductions by Blanca de los Ríos, all in Vol. I of the *Obras dramáticas completas*.

2. Bruce W. Wardropper, *Introducción al teatro religioso del Siglo de Oro*, 2nd ed. (Salamanca: Anaya, 1967), p. 323.
3. The *Diccionario de autoridades*, under "Arrendar," explains the saying as "frase que se suele usar para significar que alguno está en peligro, o expuesto a algún trabajo o castigo por algún hecho o dicho."
4. *Lecciones sobre Tirso de Molina*, pp. 50–51.
5. *Introducción al teatro religioso del Siglo de Oro*, p. 324.
6. *L'œuvre en prose de Tirso de Molina*, pp. 359–60.
7. See the prologue by L. C. Viada y Lluch to his edition of *El bandolero* (Barcelona, 1915).
8. *L'œuvre en prose de Tirso de Molina*, pp. 159–71. See also Gerald E. Wade, "Tirso's, *Cigarrales de Toledo:* Some Clarifications and Identifications," *Hispanic Review* 33 (1965), 246–72.
9. For instance, Tecla of *La patrona de las musas* comes to love St. Paul platonically through having overheard him preaching, speech and hearing being the pathways of the soul, as opposed to physical passion which is conceived through the eyes (*Deleitar aprovechando* [Madrid, 1677], fols. 58, 59). Pedro Armengol of *El bandolero*, who cannot marry Laurisana, resolves to love her spiritually and thus more perfectly (fol. 239).
10. *Deleitar aprovechando* (Madrid, 1677), fols. 200–219.
11. The conversion of a novel of adventures into the life-story of a saint would not merely match Tirso's own change of outlook, it might also have been a means of bringing out material that would otherwise have come under the ban on the publication of light literature which was still operative in Castile in the early 1630s.

Chapter Eleven

1. See also Gerald E. Wade, "Vítor, Don Juan de Alarcón/y el Fraile de la Merced," *Hispanic Review* 40 (1972), 442–50, where a somewhat different interpretation of the incident is suggested.
2. *Comedias de Tirso de Molina*, ed. Cotarelo, in *Nueva biblioteca de autores españoles*, IV, lxv.
3. *Biblioteca de autores españoles*, Vol. 5.
4. See Francis C. Hayes, "The Use of Proverbs as Titles and Motives in the *Siglo de Oro* Drama: Tirso de Molina," *Hispanic Review* 7 (1939), 310–23.
5. For a general study of Tirso's humor see Esmeralda Gijón Zapata, *El humor en Tirso de Molina* (Madrid, 1959).
6. See C. B. Morris, "Metaphor in *El burlador de Sevilla*," *Romanic Review* 55 (1964), 248–55.
7. Tirso's debt to the popular tradition is well analyzed in the introductions to two anthologies of his lyric verse: Angel López, *El cancionero popular en el teatro de Tirso de Molina* (Madrid, 1958), and Tirso de Molina, *Poesías líricas*, ed. Ernesto Jareño (Madrid: Castalia, 1969).

Selected Bibliography

As most of the significant specialized criticism on Tirso de Molina is fully documented in the preceding Notes and References, this Selected Bibliography is limited to the more important editions, general studies, and works thought likely to be of interest to the non-Hispanist reader.

BIBLIOGRAPHIES

HESSE, E. W. "Catálogo bibliográfico de Tirso de Molina." In *Tirso de Molina*, Madrid: Revista Estudios, 1949, pp. 781–889. A full classified bibliography up to the year of the tercentennial, continued for some years by means of supplements in subsequent volumes of *Estudios*.

PALOMO, MARIA DEL PILAR. "Apéndice bibliográfico." In *Obras de Tirso de Molina*, vol. 2. Biblioteca de autores españoles, vol. 236. Madrid, 1970, pp. liii–lxxix. A very useful compilation, almost complete up to the late 1960s, though unfortunately not without minor inaccuracies.

POESSE, WALTER, WILLIAMSEN, VERN G. et al. *Tirso de Molina Studies. An Annotated Bibliography*. This compilation of Tirso criticism, complete to 1975, is expected to be published during 1978.

PRIMARY SOURCES

1. Modern Collections of Plays

Comedias escogidas de Fray Gabriel Téllez (El Maestro Tirso de Molina). Edited by J. E. Hartzenbusch. Biblioteca de autores españoles, vol. 5. Madrid, 1848. Contains thirty-six plays, and seven introductory essays by various scholars.

Comedias de Tirso de Molina. Edited by E. Cotarelo y Mori. 2 vols. Nueva biblioteca de autores españoles, vols. 4 and 9. Madrid, 1906, 1907. Supplements the Hartzenbusch collection. The bibliographical material in the introductions still remains very useful.

Obras dramáticas completas. Edited by Blanca de los Ríos. 3 vols. Madrid: Aguilar, 1946, 1952, 1958. The most convenient working edition. The introductions must be read with discrimination but are by no means entirely lacking in critical perception.

Obras de Tirso de Molina. Edited by María del Pilar Palomo. 6 vols. Biblioteca de autores españoles, vols. 236–39 and 242–43. Madrid, 1970, 1971. Supplements the Hartzenbusch volume with a further forty-six plays, mainly those edited by Cotarelo, but with corrected versions of the texts. Volume 236 contains a long critical introduction and a full bibliography.

2. Plays in Modern Anthologies

El burlador de Sevilla. In *Cuatro comedias*, edited by M. M. Harlan and J. M. Hill. New York: Norton, 1941.

El condenado por desconfiado. In *Teatro español del siglo de oro*, edited by Bruce W. Wardropper. New York: Scribner's, 1970.

La prudencia en la mujer. In *Selección de comedias del siglo de oro español*, edited by Alva V. Ebersole. Chapel Hill: University of North Carolina, 1973.

3. Editions of Single Plays

El amor médico and *Averígüelo Vargas*. Edited by A. Zamora Vicente and María Josefa Canellada de Zamora. Madrid: Clásicos castellanos, 1947.

Antona García. Edited by Margaret Wilson. Manchester: Manchester University Press, 1957.

Averígüelo Vargas. See above, under *El amor médico*.

El burlador de Sevilla and *El vergonzoso en palacio*. Edited by A. Castro. Madrid: Clásicos castellanos, 1922.

El burlador de Sevilla. Edited by Gerald E. Wade. New York: Scribner's, 1969.

El condenado por desconfiado. Edited by Daniel Rogers. Oxford: Pergamon, 1974.

Don Gil de las calzas verdes. Edited by Ricardo Domenech. Madrid: Taurus, 1969.

Marta la piadosa. Edited by J. Loveluck. Santiago de Chile: Zig-zag, 1956.

El melancólico. Edited by B. Varela Jácome. Madrid: Aguilar, 1967.

Por el sótano y el torno. Edited by A. Zamora Vicente. Buenos Aires: Universidad de Buenos Aires, 1949.

Privar contra su gusto. Edited by Battista Galassi. Madrid: Plaza Mayor, 1971.

La prudencia en la mujer. Edited by A. H. Bushee and L. L. Stafford. Mexico City: Mexico City College Press, 1948.

La Santa Juana. Edited by Agustín del Campo. Madrid: Castilla, 1948.

La venganza de Tamar. Edited by A. K. G. Paterson. Cambridge: Cambridge University Press, 1969.

El vergonzoso en palacio. See above, under *El burlador de Sevilla*.

El vergonzoso en palacio. Edited by Francisco Ayala. Madrid: Castalia, 1971.

Selected Bibliography

4. Editions of Other Works

Los cigarrales de Toledo. Edited by V. Said Armesto. Madrid: Renacimiento, 1613.

Los cigarrales de Toledo. 2 vols. Madrid: Espasa-Calpe, 1942.

Deleitar aprovechando. There is no modern edition of the whole of this work, but two of its stories have been separately edited: *El bandolero.* Edited by L. Viada y Lluch. Barcelona: Pugés, 1915; and *La patrona de las musas.* Edited by R. Froldi. Milan: Istituto Editoriale Cisalpino, 1959.

Historia general de la Orden de Nuestra Señora de las Mercedes. Edited by Manuel Penedo Rey. 2 vols. Madrid: Provincia de la Merced de Castilla, Colección Revista Estudios, 1973, 1974.

5. Translations of *El Burlador de Sevilla*

The Love Rogue. Translated by Harry Kemp. New York: Lieber and Lewis, 1923.

The Rogue of Seville. Translated by Robert O'Brien. In *Spanish Drama*, edited by A. Flores. New York: Bantam Books, 1962. An adequate prose version.

The Trickster of Seville. Translated by Roy Campbell. In *Masterpieces of the Spanish Golden Age*, edited by A. Flores. New York: Holt, Rinehart and Winston, 1957. A rendering in verse, slightly free, but faithful to the spirit of the original.

SECONDARY SOURCES

1. General Works on Golden Age Drama

MCKENDRICK, MELVEENA. *Woman and Society in the Spanish Drama of the Golden Age: a Study of the 'Mujer varonil'.* Cambridge: Cambridge University Press, 1974. A study of various types of forceful female characters, including examination of nine plays by Tirso in which such figures appear.

PARKER, A. A. *The Approach to the Spanish Drama of the Golden Age.* London: Hispanic and Luso-Brazilian Councils, 1957. Reprinted in revised form as "The Spanish Drama of the Golden Age: a Method of Analysis and Interpretation," in *The Great Playwrights*, edited by Eric Bentley, vol. 1 (New York: Garden City, 1970). A short but indispensable analysis of the principles underlying much of Golden Age drama.

REICHENBERGER, ARNOLD G. "The Uniqueness of the *Comedia.*" *Hispanic Review* 27 (1959), 303–16. A characterization of Spanish Golden Age drama, stressing its themes of honor and faith. Supplemented by another article with the same title, *Hispanic Review* 38 (1970), 163–73.

SHERGOLD, N. D. *A History of the Spanish Stage.* Oxford: Oxford University Press, 1967. A detailed and masterly study of the staging of Spanish plays up to the end of the seventeenth century.

WILSON, EDWARD M., and MOIR, DUNCAN. *The Golden Age: Drama 1492–1700* (one volume of *A Literary History of Spain*). London: Benn, 1971. An impressively comprehensive account of Golden Age drama.

WILSON, MARGARET. *Spanish Drama of the Golden Age*. Oxford: Pergamon, 1969. An analytical survey of Golden Age drama and its development.

2. General Studies of Tirso

AGHEANA, ION TUDOR. *The Situational Drama of Tirso de Molina*. New York: Plaza Mayor, 1972. A quest for Tirso's artistic individuality, seen in a movement away from convention toward "situational reality."

KENNEDY, RUTH LEE. *Studies in Tirso, I: the Dramatist and his Competitors, 1620–26*. North Carolina Studies in Romance Languages and Literatures. Chapel Hill, 1974. The first of a projected series of three volumes. Although each of the studies treats a specialized subject, together they constitute a masterly presentation of Tirso during his years of major literary activity.

MCCLELLAND, I. L. *Tirso de Molina: Studies in Dramatic Realism*. Liverpool: Institute of Hispanic Studies, 1948. An analysis of the psychological realism of some Tirsian characters. A stimulating book, which always bears stage performance in mind, but which unfortunately relies on some plays of doubtful authorship.

MANCINI, GUIDO, et al. *Studi tirsiani*. Milan: Feltrinelli, 1958. Six essays in Italian by different scholars, one general and the others on individual works.

MAUREL, SERGE. *L'univers dramatique de Tirso de Molina*. Poitiers: Université de Poitiers, 1971. The thesis of this work, that the whole of Tirso's theater shares the same Christian orientation, is debatable, but the book as a whole offers the fullest and most profound analysis of Tirso's drama so far.

SULLIVAN, HENRY W. *Tirso de hislina and the Drama of the Counter Reformation*. Amsterdam: Rodopi, 1976. A stimulating attempt to place Tirsian drama against the background of neo-Scholastic theology.

VOSSLER, KARL. *Lecciones sobre Tirso de Molina*. Madrid: Taurus, 1965. Lectures originally given in 1938, and now somewhat outdated, but still offering some useful insights.

Index

Agheana, Ion Tudor, 150n4 to Chapter 7
Alcalá de Henares, 21, 65
allegory, 106–107, 126–29
Almazán, 29
Anderson, Robert R., 119, 150ch8n4
Arcadia, La (Lope de Vega), 53, 54, 55, 140
Arróniz, O., 148n1 to Chapter 3
As You Like It (Shakespeare), 45, 48–49, 67
Asensio, Jaime, 72, 107, 108, 151n7
Aubrun, C. V., 152n10
autos sacramentales, 28, 106, *126–29*, 130, 131
Ayala, Francisco, 48

banditry, 118–19, 131, 134
Barcelona, 17, 36
Basque country, 92–93
Bible, biblical material, 71–72, 80–81, 92, 103–108, 142
Blois, Louis de (Blosius, Ludovicus), 116
Boccaccio, 130, 132
Bruerton, Courtney, 43, 44
burla, 122, 123, 130

Calderón, Pedro, 13, 24, 31, 34, 79, 84, 85, 126, 127, 129, 143, 149ch5n4
Calderón, Rodrigo, 87
Canellada de Zamora, María Josefa, 149n1 to Chapter 5
Casalduero, J., 152n16
Castro, Guillén de, 24
Catalonia, 17, 18, 28, 131
Cervantes, 69, 131, 135
Claramonte, Andrés de, 114

comendador theme, 100–102
conceits. *See* imagery
Cotarelo, E., 14, 39, 146n4, 152n10
Cuenca, 28, 29
culto language, 44, 70, 89, 101, 105, 114, 132, 140

Decameron (Boccaccio), 130
Dellepiane, Angela B., 146n16
"discoveries". *See* staging
Duke of Viseu, The (Lope de Vega), 94, 95

edict of Committee for Reform, 25–26, 27, 35, 61, 69, 136
Elliott, J. H., 124–25, 146n17, 150ch7n1

Feydeau, 78
Fianza satisfecha, La (?Lope de Vega), 119, 150ch8n4
Fieras afemina amor (Calderón), 149n4 to Chapter 5
Figueroa, Roque de, 114
Filocolo (Boccaccio), 132
Franco de Guzmán, Pedro, 26
Froldi, R., 148n2
Fuenteovejuna (Lope de Vega), 58, 61, 95, 100, 101

Galicia, 60, 61, 65, 149ch4n5
Gijón Zapata, Esmeralda, 153ch11n5
Góngora, 24, 44, 53, 70, 105, 132, 136, 140
González, Jaime José, 83
Guadalajara, 21, 24, 27, 64, 65, 134
Guastavino, Guillermo, 17

159

Halkhoree, P., 64, 148n7
Hayes, Francis C., 153ch11n4
Hesse, Everett W., 149ch5n3
honor, 78–81, 100, 122, 123, 128–29, 136
Hurtado de Mendoza, Antonio, 26, 137

imagery, 55, 72, 79, 82, 83, 84, 105, 107, 110, 113, 128, 132, 134, 139, 140–41
Italian and Italianate comedy, 30, 45, 57, 67

Jareño, E., 153ch11n7
Jones, Cyril A., 149ch5n6
Jones, R. O., 58
Julius Casesar (Shakespeare), 96

Kennedy, Ruth Lee, 18, 19, 20, 26, 38, 39, 41, 42, 43, 44, 53, 82, 84, 88, 91, 92, 105, 108, 115, 117, 137, 147n7, 149ch5n2, 151n6
King Lear (Shakespeare), 84

Lerma, duke of, 22, 25, 62, 87, 88
Lopean drama, 30–34, 66, 98
López, Angel, 153ch11n7
Lucas de Avila, Francisco, 18, 36, 37, 38, 39

Macbeth (Shakespeare), 112
McCrary, William C., 149ch5n3
McKendrick, Melveena, 152n23
Madrid, 13, 14, 18, 19, 20, 21, 24, 26, 27, 28, 31, 35, 36, 37, 39, 49, 51, 52, 55, 57, 58, 62, 63, 64, 65, 86, 88, 96, 106, 114, 127, 130, 136, 142
Maurel, Serge, 65, 99, 116, 121, 149n9, 149ch5n1, 150n7 to Chapter 7, 150ch8n2, n5 and n6
Mayberry, Robert J., 151n3
Médico de su honra, El (Calderón), 79
Menéndez Pidal, R., 152n10
Mercedarian order, 13, 18, 20, 21, 27, 28, 29, 101, 133
Merchant of Venice, The (Shakespeare), 45
metaphors. *See* imagery
meters, 43, 82, 92, 105, 132, 147n18
Metford, J. C. J., 106, 108

Mira de Amescua, Antonio, 24, 38, 39, 84, 136
Moir, D. W., 93
Molina de Aragón, 18
Moll, Jaime, 35, 36
Montalbán, Juan Pérez de, 139, 142
Morley, S. G., 43, 147n18
Morris, C. B., 153ch11n6
Much Ado About Nothing (Shakespeare), 45
Muñoz Peña, Pedro, 14

Neoplatonism, 52, 75, 132
Nougué, André, 19, 43, 44, 129, 130, 131

Olivares, count-duke of, 25, 26, 27, 28, 29, 42, 51, 53, 83, 86, 87, 88, 90, 91, 108, 137
Orlando furioso (Ariosto), 59
Osuna, duke of, 15, 16

Parker, A. A., 119, 121
Paterson, A. K. G., 81, 115
Penedo Rey, Manuel, 15, 17, 18, 19, 20, 21, 26, 27, 29, 37, 38, 133, 145n7
Penna, Mario, 16
Peregrino en su patria, El (Lope de Vega), 131
Pérez, Carlos A., 152n21
Peribáñez (Lope de Vega), 59–60, 100, 105
Persiles y Sigismunda (Cervantes), 131
Philip III, 20, 22, 25, 42, 53, 87, 88
Philip IV, 25, 42, 87, 90, 91, 92
Placer, Gumersindo, 149ch4n5
Platonism. *See* Neoplatonism
Portugal, the Portuguese, 46, 60, 61, 68, 87, 94, 95
privados, privanza, 25, 83, 86–92, 108, 115, 123, 128, 129, 142
publication of Golden Age plays, 34–35

Quevedo, 24, 69, 140
Quiñones de Benavente, Luis, 38

Reina de los reyes, La (Hipólito de Vergara), 38
Remón, Alonso, 28, 40

Index

rhetoric, 70, 79, 140
Ríos, Blanca de los, 14, 15, 16, 18, 19, 20, 43, 51, 56, 61, 70, 76, 98, 103, 112, 116, 138, 152n1
Ríos, Miguel L., 15
Rogers, Daniel, 114, 116, 117, 119, 121, 124, 151n2
Ruiz de Alarcón, Juan, 24, 84, 137
Rus Lucenilla, José, 16

Salamanca, 21, 27
Salmerón, Marcos, 28, 29
Salomon, Noël, 58, 59, 150ch8n5
Santo Domingo, 23, 24, 29, 32, 134; *see also* West Indies
satire, 52, 53, 55, 61, 69, 75, 78, 105, 108, 139, 140
Segovia, 21, 24, 29, 58, 65
Semiramis, 85, 93, 94, 96, 104
Seville, 27, 35, 36, 41, 58, 65, 67, 109, 110, 113, 114, 121, 122, 124
Shakespeare, William, 45, 67, 84, 95, 96, 112, 141
Shergold, N. D., 148n10, 149ch4n6
Sloman, Albert E., 151n3
Soria, 29
staging, 93, 94, 105, 106, 124
Sullivan, Henry, 16–17
symbolism, 64, 90, 105, 107, 117–18, 123, 142, 143

Taming of the Shrew, The (Shakespeare), 45
Téllez, Gabriel. *See* Tirso de Molina
Tempest, The (Shakespeare), 45
Thirty Years' War, 42
Tirso de Molina: autobiographical allusions in plays, 26, 56, 69, 76, 86, 96–97, 138; censured by Salmerón, 28–29; date of birth, 13–17; death, 29; dramatic career, 21–23, 24–25; enmities, 19, 26, 39, 86, 136, 137, 138; family, 17–20; libeled by *vítor*, 137; Mercedarian monk, 20–21, 23–24, 27–29; relations with Lope, 22, 32–33, 54, 136; role in controversy over drama, 32–34; silenced by edict, 25–26

WORKS—DRAMA:
Achilles, The, 69–71, 86, 138, 139, 140
Amor médico, El. See Love Turned Doctor
Amor y celos hacen discretos. See Love and Jealousy Make Men Wise
Amor y el amistad, El. See Love and Friendship
Antona García, 26, 54, 61, 94–97, 101, 113, 136
Aquiles, El. See Achilles, The
Arms of Portugal, The, 42
Burlador de Sevilla, El. See Trickster of Seville, The
Caballero de Gracia, El, 42
Castigo del penséque, El. See Penalty for 'Thinking That,' The
Cautela contra cautela. See Cunning Matched with Cunning
Celosa de sí misma, La. See Jealous of Herself
Celoso prudente, El. See Jealous but Prudent
Colmenero divino, El. See Divine Beekeeper, The
Cómo han de ser los amigos. See True Friendship
Condenado por desconfiado, El. See Man of Little Faith, The
Cretan Labyrinth, The, 126
Cunning Matched with Cunning, 39, 84
Dama del olivar, La. See Lady of the Olive Grove, The
Divine Beekeeper, The, 127–28
Don Gil de las calzas verdes. See Don Gil of the Green Breeches
Don Gil of the Green Breeches, 22, 41, 49–51, 62, 67, 139, 140, 141
Elección por la virtud, La. See Elected for his Virtue
Elected for his Virtue, 41, 98–100, 113
Enough is as Good as a Feast, 41, 105–108, 117, 140
Esto sí que es negociar. See That's Business!
Feigned Arcady, 42, 53–56, 57, 63, 68, 83, 140

Fingida Arcadia, La. See *Feigned Arcady*
Fortune in a Name, 68
Galician Mari-Hernández, The, 60–62, 66, 69, 94, 113
Gallega Mari-Hernández, La. See *Galician Mari-Hernández, The*
Greatest Disillusion, The, 115
Heavenly Sponsor, The, 126–27
Hermanos parecidos, Los. See *Identical Brothers, The*
Identical Brothers, The, 42, 127, 128
Jealous but Prudent, 33, 42, 78–80, 81, 82, 84, 88, 138, 140
Jealous of Herself, 51–53, 63, 66, 89, 140
Laberinto de Creta, El. See *Cretan Labyrinth, The*
Lady of the Olive Grove, The, 101–102, 113, 119
Love and Friendship, 39, 82–84, 88
Love and Jealousy Make Men Wise, 38, 41
Love Turned Doctor, 39, 67–69, 94, 139
Madrina del cielo, La. See *Heavenly Sponsor, The*
Man of Little Faith, The, 39, 40, 110–25
Marta la piadosa. See *Pious Martha*
Mayor desengaño, El. See *Greatest Disillusion, The*
Melancholic, The, 38, 74–75, 76, 77, 78, 79, 88, 114, 138, 140, 142
Melancólico, El. See *Melancholic, The*
Much good may it do him!, 127, 128–29
Mujer por fuerza, La. See *Woman Against her Will, A*
Mujer que manda en casa, La. See *Wife who Rules the Roost, The*
No le arriendo la ganancia. See *Much good may it do him!*
Palabras y plumas. See *Words and Feathers*
Penalty for 'Thinking That,' The, 138
Peña de Francia, La. See *Rock of France, The*

Pious Martha, 22, 42, 62–63, 66, 139, 140, 141
Pizarro trilogy, 42
Por el sótano y el torno. See *Through Basement and Hatch*
Privar contra su gusto. See *Reluctant Favorite, The*
Prudence in Woman, 18, 42, 90–94, 95, 96, 108, 116
Prudencia en la mujer, La. See *Prudence in Woman*
Quien no cae no se levanta. See *Who Never Falls Never Rises*
Quinas de Portugal, Las. See *Arms of Portugal, The*
Reluctant Favorite, The, 42, 84, 88–90, 108, 140, 142
Rock of France, The, 98–100
Saber guardar su hacienda, 105
Santa Juana trilogy, 40, 41, 42, 58, 98–101, 113, 114
Shy Man at Court, The, 21, 22, 32–33, 42, 46–49, 50, 56, 62, 66, 85, 87, 94, 98, 139, 140, 141
Tamar's Vengeance, 43, 71–74, 78, 80–81, 85, 103, 108, 113, 117, 141, 142–43
¡Tan largo me lo fiáis! See *What Long Credit You Give me!*
Tanto es lo de más como lo de menos. See *Enough is as Good as a Feast*
That's Business!, 38, 74–75, 142
Through Basement and Hatch, 38, 63–65, 69, 139, 142
Trickster of Seville, The, 39, 40, 109–25, 128, 141, 142
True Friendship, 18, 41. 81–82, 83, 84, 85, 87, 139
Venganza de Tamar, La. See *Tamar's Vengeance*
Ventura con el nombre, La. See *Fortune in a Name*
Vergonzoso en palacio, El. See *Shy Man at Court, The*
Village Girl from Vallecas, The, 42, 88
Village Girl of La Sagra, The, 58–60, 61, 62, 72, 139
Villana de la Sagra, La. See *Village Girl of La Sagra, The*

Index

Villana de Vallecas, La. See *Village Girl from Vallecas, The*
What Long Credit You Give Me!, 112–14, 142
Who Never Falls Never Rises, 102–103, 107, 113, 140
Wife who Rules the Roost, The, 103–105, 107, 108, 142–43
Woman Against her Will, A, 39
Words and Feathers, 84
WORKS—PROSE:
Bandit, The, 131, 132, 133, 134, 138
Bandolero, El. See *Bandit, The*
Cigarrales de Toledo, Los. See *Country Houses of Toledo, The*
Country Houses of Toledo, The, 18, 19, 21, 22, 24, 26, 27, 28, 32–33, 34, 35, 36, 39, 40, 49, 54, 55, 76, 80, 81, 82, 83, 87, 94, 129–33, 136
Deleitar aprovechando. See *Pleasure with Profit*
History of the Mercedarian Order, 17, 21, 23, 27, 28, 29, 88, 133–35
Life of Santa María de Cervellón, 17, 28
Patron of the Muses, The, 130–31
Patrona de las musas, La. See *Patron of the Muses, The*
Pleasure with Profit, 17, 23, 27–28, 42, 126, 127, 129–33
Triumphs of Truth, The, 131, 132
Triunfos de la verdad, Los. See *Triumphs of Truth, The*
WORKS—VERSE:
Act of Contrition, 27, 37, 130, 137
Toledo, Toledan years, 19, 20, 21, 22, 23, 29, 41, 58, 59, 60, 62, 63, 65, 127, 128, 130, 136, 142

Tortosa, 36
tramoyas, 53, 55, 56, 61, 100, 140
Trujillo, 27, 42
Twelfth Night (Shakespeare), 45, 57, 67
Two Gentlemen of Verona (Shakespeare), 45

Uceda, duke of, 87

Valdés, Pedro de, 41
Valencia, 35, 36, 45
Valenciano twins, 42, 128
Varey, J. E., 149ch4n6
Vega, Lope de, 13, 22, 23, 24, 26, 30, 31, 32, 33, 34, 35, 38, 41, 44, 45, 49, 50, 53, 54, 57, 58, 59, 61, 66, 94, 95, 100, 102, 103, 105, 126, 131, 136, 140, 141, 143
Vélez de Guevara, Luis, 24, 53, 137
Viada y Lluch, L. C., 153ch10n7
Vossler, Karl, 98, 129

Wade, Gerald E., 16, 19, 22, 23, 44, 83, 88, 114, 146n12, 151n3, 153n1
Wardropper, Bruce W., 127, 129, 152n24
Weiger, John G., 148n2
West Indies, 14, 17, 23–24, 41, 63, 101: *see also* Santo Domingo
Whitby, William M., 119, 150ch8n4
Wilson, Margaret, 146n18, 147n7, 148n6, 149ch6n1, 150ch7n6
Winter's Tale, The (Shakespeare), 45

Zamora Vicente, Alonso, 149ch5n1